THE ART OF LIVING

VIPASSANA MEDITATION

AS TAUGHT BY
S. N. GOENKA

William Hart

HarperOne
An Imprint of HarperCollinsPublishers

HarperOne

Grateful acknowledgment is made for permission to adapt from *Vipassana Journal*, (speccial commemorative issue), the Vipashyana Research Institute, Bombay; from the *Vipassana Newsletter*, Vol. XII, Nos. 1, 3. and 4, Vol. XIII, No. 1, Shelburne Falls, MA; from "Pure Mind: Exploring the Path of Enlightenment," interview with S. N. Goenka conducted by Steve Minkin, copyright © 1982 by East West Journal, reprinted by permission of the publisher.

Preface copyright © 1987 by S. N. Goenka.

THE ART OF LIVING. Copyright © 1987 by William Hart. All rights reserved. Printed in the United States of America. No part of this book may be used or reproduced in any manner whatsoever without written permission except in the case of brief quotations embodied in critical articles and reviews. For information address HarperCollins Publishers, 195 Broadway, New York, NY 10007.

HarperCollins books may be purchased for educational, business, or sales promotional use. For information, please e-mail the Special Markets Department at SPsales@harpercollins.com.

HarperCollins Web site: http://www.harpercollins.com

HarperCollins®, 📖®, and HarperOne™ are trademarks of HarperCollins Publishers.

Library of Congress Cataloging-in-Publication Data
Hart, William.
  The art of living.

  1. Vipaśyanà (Buddhism).   2. Goenka, S. N.   3. Religious life
  (Buddhism).   I. Title.
BQ5630.V5H37   1987
294.3'443   86–45810
ISBN: 978–0–06–063724–8

Wisdom is the principal thing;
therefore get wisdom:
and with all thy getting
get understanding.

Proverbs, iv. 7. (KJV)

CONTENTS

FOREWORD

I am forever grateful for the change that Vipassana meditation has wrought in my life. When I first learned this technique I felt as though I had been wandering in a maze of blind alleys and now at last had found the royal road. In the years since then I have kept following this road, and with every step the goal has become clearer: liberation from all suffering, full enlightenment. I cannot claim to have reached the final goal, but I have no doubt that this way leads directly there.

For showing me this way I am always indebted to Sayagyi U Ba Khin and to the chain of teachers who kept the technique alive through millennia from the time of the Buddha. On behalf of them all I encourage others to take this road, so that they also may find the way out of suffering.

Although many thousands of people from Western countries have learned it, up to now no book has appeared that accurately describes this form of Vipassana at length. I am pleased that at last a serious meditator has undertaken to fill this gap.

May this book deepen the understanding of those who practice Vipassana meditation, and may it encourage others to try this technique so that they too may experience the happiness of liberation. May every reader learn the art of living in order to find peace and harmony within and to generate peace and harmony for others.

May all beings be happy!

S. N. GOENKA

Bombay
April 1986

PREFACE

Among the various types of meditation in the world today, the Vipassana method taught by S. N. Goenka is unique. This technique is a simple, logical way to achieve real peace of mind and to lead a happy, useful life. Long preserved within the Buddhist community in Burma, Vipassana itself contains nothing of a sectarian nature, and can be accepted and applied by people of any background.

S. N. Goenka is a retired industrialist, and a former leader of the Indian community in Burma. Born into a conservative Hindu family, he suffered from youth onward from severe migraine headaches. His search for a cure brought him into contact in 1955 with Sayagyi U Ba Khin, who combined the public role of a senior civil servant with the private role of a teacher of meditation. In learning Vipassana from U Ba Khin, Mr. Goenka found a discipline that went far beyond alleviating the symptoms of physical disease and transcended cultural and religious barriers. Vipassana gradually transformed his life in the ensuing years of practice and study under the guidance of his teacher.

In 1969 Mr. Goenka was authorized as a teacher of Vipassana meditation by U Ba Khin. In that year he came to India and began teaching Vipassana there, reintroducing this technique into the land of its origin. In a country still sharply divided by caste and religion, Mr. Goenka's courses have attracted thousands of people of every background. Thousands of Westerners have also participated in Vipassana courses, attracted by the practical nature of the technique.

The qualities of Vipassana are exemplified by Mr. Goenka himself. He is a pragmatic person, in touch with the ordinary realities of life and able to deal with them incisively, but in every situation he maintains an extraordinary calmness of mind. Along with that calmness is a deep compassion for others, an ability to empathize with virtually any human being. There is, however, nothing solemn about him. He has an engaging sense of humor which he exercises in his teaching. Course participants long remember his smile, his laughter, and his often-repeated motto, "Be happy!" Clearly Vipassana has brought him happiness, and he is eager to share that happiness with others by showing them the technique that has worked so well for him.

Despite his magnetic presence, Mr. Goenka has no wish to be a guru who turns his disciples into automatons. Instead he teaches self-responsibility. The real test of Vipassana, he says, is applying it in life. He encourages meditators not to sit at his feet, but to go out and live happily in the world. He shuns all expressions of devotion to him, instead directing his students to be devoted to the technique, to the truth that they find within themselves.

In Burma it has traditionally been the prerogative of Buddhist monks to teach meditation. Like his teacher, however, Mr. Goenka is a layman and is the head of a large family. Nevertheless, the clarity of his teaching and the efficacy of the technique itself have won the approval of senior monks in Burma, India, and Sri Lanka, a number of whom have taken courses under his guidance.

To maintain its purity, Mr. Goenka insists, meditation must never become a business. Courses and centers operating under his direction are all run on a totally nonprofit basis. He himself receives no remuneration for his work directly or indirectly, nor do the assistant teachers whom he has authorized to teach courses as his representatives. He distributes the technique of Vipassana purely as a service to humanity, to help those who are in need of help.

S. N. Goenka is one of the few Indian spiritual leaders as highly respected in India as in the West. However, he has never sought publicity, preferring to rely on word of mouth to spread interest in Vipassana; and he has always emphasized the importance of actual meditation practice over mere writings about meditation. For these reasons he is less widely known than he deserves to be. This book is the first full-length study of his teaching prepared under his guidance and with his approval.

The principal source materials for this work are the discourses given by Mr. Goenka during a ten-day Vipassana course and, to a lesser extent, his written articles in English. I have used these materials freely, borrowing not only lines of argument and organization of specific points, but also examples given in the discourses, and frequently exact wording, even entire sentences. To those who have participated in Vipassana meditation courses as taught by him, much of this book will certainly be familiar, and they may even be able to identify the particular discourse or article that has been used at a certain point in the text.

During a course, the explanations of the teacher are accompanied step by step by the experience of the participants in meditation. Here the material has been reorganized for the benefit of a different audience, people who are merely reading about meditation without necessarily having practiced it. For such readers an attempt has been made to present the teaching as it is actually experienced: a logical progression flowing unbroken from the first step to the final goal. That organic wholeness is most easily apparent to the meditator, but this work tries to provide non-meditators with a glimpse of the teaching as it unfolds to one who practices it.

Certain sections deliberately preserve the tone of the spoken word in order to convey a more vivid impression of the way in which Mr. Goenka teaches. These sections are the stories set between the chapters and the questions and answers that conclude each chapter, dialogues taken from actual discussions with students during a course or in private interviews. Some of the stories are drawn from events in the life of the Buddha, others from the rich Indian heritage of folk tales, and others still from the personal experiences of Mr. Goenka. All are narrated in his own words, not with the intention of improving on the originals but simply to present the stories in a fresh way, emphasizing their relevance to the practice of meditation. These stories lighten the serious atmosphere of a Vipassana course and offer inspiration by illustrating central points of the teaching in memorable form. Of the many such stories told in a ten-day course, only a small selection has been included here.

Quotations are from the oldest and most widely accepted record of the Buddha's words, the *Discourse Collection* (*Sutta Piṭaka*), as it has been preserved in the ancient Pāli language in Theravadin Buddhist countries. To maintain a uniform tone throughout the book, I have attempted to translate afresh all the passages quoted here. In doing so I have taken guidance from the work of leading modern translators. However, since this is not a scholarly work, I have not striven to achieve word-for-word accuracy in translating the Pāli. Instead I have tried to convey in straightforward language the sense of each passage as it appears to a Vipassana meditator in the light of his meditation experience. Perhaps the rendering of certain words or passages may seem unorthodox, but in matters of substance, I hope, the English follows the most literal meaning of the original texts.

For the sake of consistency and precision, Buddhist terms used in the text have been given in their Pāli forms even though in some cases the Sanskrit may be more familiar to readers of English. For example, the Pāli **dhamma** is used in place of the Sanskrit *dharma,* **kamma** instead of *karma,* **nibbāna** instead of *nirvāṇa,* **sankhāra** instead of *samskāra.* To make the text easier to understand, Pāli words have been pluralized in English style, by adding *s.* In general, Pāli words in the text have been kept to a minimum to avoid unnecessary obscurity. However, they often offer a convenient shorthand for certain concepts unfamiliar to Western thought which cannot easily be expressed in a single word in English. For this reason, at points it has seemed preferable to use the Pāli rather than a longer English phrase. All Pāli forms printed in boldface type are defined in the glossary at the back of this book.

The technique of Vipassana offers equal benefits to all who practice it, without any discrimination on the basis of race, class, or sex. In order to remain faithful to this universal approach, I have tried to avoid using sexually exclusive language in the text. At points, however, I have used the pronoun "he" to refer to a meditator of unspecified gender. Readers are asked to consider the usage as sexually indeterminate. There is no intention of excluding women or giving undue prominence to men, since such a partiality would be contrary to the basic teaching and spirit of Vipassana.

I am grateful to the many who helped on this project. In particular, I wish to express my deep gratitude to S. N. Goenka for taking time from his busy schedule to look over the work as it developed, and even more for guiding me to take a few beginning steps on the path described here.

In a deeper sense, the true author of this work is S. N. Goenka, since my purpose is simply to present his transmission of the teaching of the Buddha. The merits of this work belong to him. Whatever defects exist are my own responsibility.

INTRODUCTION

Suppose you had the opportunity to free yourself of all worldly responsibilities for ten days, with a quiet, secluded place in which to live, protected from disturbances. In this place the basic physical requirements of room and board would be provided for you, and helpers would be on hand to see that you were reasonably comfortable. In return you would be expected only to avoid contact with others and, apart from essential activities, to spend all your waking hours with eyes closed, keeping your mind on a chosen object of attention. Would you accept the offer?

Suppose you had simply heard that such an opportunity existed, and that people like yourself were not only willing but eager to spend their free time in this way. How would you describe their activity? Navel-gazing, you might say, or contemplation; escapism or spiritual retreat; self-intoxication or self-searching; introversion or introspection. Whether the connotation is negative or positive, the common impression of meditation is that it is a withdrawal from the world. Of course there are techniques that function in this way. But meditation need not be an escape. It can also be a means to encounter the world in order to understand it and ourselves.

Every human being is conditioned to assume that the real world is outside, that the way to live life is by contact with an external reality, by seeking input, physical and mental, from without. Most of us have never considered severing outward contacts in order to see what happens inside. The idea of doing so probably sounds like choosing to spend hours staring at the test pattern on a television screen. We would rather explore the far side of the moon or the bottom of the ocean than the hidden depths within ourselves.

But in fact the universe exists for each of us only when we experience it with body and mind. It is never elsewhere, it is always here and now. By exploring the here-and-now of ourselves we can explore the world. Unless we investigate the world within we can never know reality—we will only know our beliefs about it, or our intellectual conceptions of it. By observing ourselves, however, we can come to know reality directly and can learn to deal with it in a positive, creative way.

One method of exploring the inner world is Vipassana meditation as taught by S. N. Goenka. This is a practical way to examine the reality of one's own body and mind, to uncover and solve whatever problems lie hidden there, to develop unused potential, and to channel it for one's own good and the good of others.

Vipassanā means "insight" in the ancient Pāli language of India. It is the essence of the teaching of the Buddha, the actual experience of the truths of which he spoke. The Buddha himself attained that experience by the practice of meditation, and therefore meditation is what he primarily taught. His words are records of his experiences in meditation, as well as detailed instructions on how to practice in order to reach the goal he had attained, the experience of truth.

This much is widely accepted, but the problem remains of how to understand and follow the instructions given by the Buddha. While his words have been preserved in texts of recognized authenticity, the interpretation of his meditation instructions is difficult without the context of a living practice. But if a technique exists that has been maintained for unknown generations, that offers the very results described by the Buddha, and if it conforms precisely to his instructions and elucidates points in them that have long seemed obscure, then that technique is surely worth investigating. Vipassana is such a method. It is a technique extraordinary in its simplicity, its lack of all dogma, and above all in the results it offers.

But if a technique exists that has been maintained for unknown generations, that offers the very results described by the Buddha, and if it conforms precisely to his instructions and elucidates points in them that have long seemed obscure, then that technique is surely worth investigating. Vipassana is such a method. It is a technique extraordinary in its simplicity, its lack of all dogma, and above all in the results it offers.

Vipassana meditation is taught in courses of ten days, open to anyone who sincerely wishes to learn the technique and who is fit to do so physically and mentally. During the ten days, participants remain within the area of the course site, having no contact with the outside world. They refrain from reading and writing, and suspend any religious or other practices, working exactly according to the instructions given. For the entire period of the course they follow a basic code of morality which includes celibacy and abstention from all intoxicants. They also maintain silence among themselves for the first nine days of the course, although they are free to discuss meditation problems with the teacher and material problems with the management.

During the first three and a half days the participants practice an exercise of mental concentration. This is preparatory to the technique of Vipassana proper, which is introduced on the fourth day of the course. Further steps within the practice are introduced each day, so that by the end of the course the entire technique has been presented in outline. On the tenth day silence ends, and meditators make the transition back to a more extroverted way of life. The course concludes on the morning of the eleventh day.

The experience of ten days is likely to contain a number of surprises for the meditator. The first is that meditation is hard work! The popular idea that it is a kind of inactivity or relaxation is soon found to be a misconception. Continual application is needed to direct the mental processes consciously in a particular way. The instructions are to work with full effort yet without any tension, but until one learns how to do this, the exercise can be frustrating or even exhausting.

Another surprise is that, to begin with, the insights gained by self-observation are not likely to be all pleasant and blissful. Normally we are very selective in our view of ourselves. When we look into a mirror we are careful to strike the most flattering pose, the most pleasing expression. In the same way we each have a mental image of ourselves which emphasizes admirable qualities, minimizes defects, and omits some sides of our character altogether. We see the image that we wish to see, not the reality. But Vipassana meditation is a technique for observing reality from every angle. Instead of a carefully edited self-image, the meditator confronts the whole uncensored truth. Certain aspects of it are bound to be hard to accept.

At times it may seem that instead of finding inner peace one has found nothing but agitation by meditating. Everything about the course may seem unworkable, unacceptable: the heavy timetable, the facilities, the discipline, the instructions and advice of the teacher, the technique itself.

Another surprise, however, is that the difficulties pass away. At a certain point meditators learn to make effortless efforts, to maintain a relaxed alertness, a detached involvement. Instead of struggling, they become engrossed in the practice. Now inadequacies of the facilities seem unimportant, the discipline becomes a helpful support, the hours pass quickly, unnoticed. The mind becomes as calm as a mountain lake at dawn, perfectly mirroring its surroundings and at the same time revealing its depths to those who look more closely. When this clarity comes, every moment is full of affirmation, beauty, and peace.

Thus the meditator discovers that the technique actually works. Each step in turn may seem an enormous leap, and yet one finds one can do it. At the end of ten days it becomes clear how long a journey it has been from the beginning of the course. The meditator has undergone a process analogous to a surgical operation, to lancing a pus-filled wound. Cutting open the lesion and pressing on it to remove the pus is painful, but unless this is done the wound can never heal. Once the pus is removed, one is free of it and of the suffering it caused, and can regain full health. Similarly, by passing through a ten-day course, the meditator relieves the mind of some of its tensions, and enjoys greater mental health. The process of Vipassana has worked deep changes within, changes that persist after the end of the course. The meditator finds that whatever mental strength was gained during the course, whatever was learned, can be applied in daily life for one's own benefit and for the good of others. Life becomes more harmonious, fruitful, and happy.

The technique taught by S. N. Goenka is that which he learned from his teacher, the late Sayagyi U Ba Khin of Burma, who was taught Vipassana by Saya U Thet, a well-known teacher of meditation in Burma in the first half of this century. In turn, Saya U Thet was a pupil of Ledi Sayadaw, a famous Burmese scholar-monk of the late nineteenth and early twentieth centuries. Further back there is no record of the names of the teachers of this technique, but it is believed by those who practice it that Ledi Sayadaw learned Vipassana meditation from traditional teachers who had preserved it through generations since ancient times, when the teaching of the Buddha was first introduced into Burma.

Certainly the technique agrees with the instructions of the Buddha on meditation, with the simplest, most literal meaning of his words. And most important, it provides results that are good, personal, tangible, and immediate.

This book is not a do-it-yourself manual for the practice of Vipassana meditation, and people who use it this way proceed entirely at their own risk. The technique should be learned only in a course where there is a proper environment to support the meditator and a properly trained guide. Meditation is a serious matter, especially the Vipassana technique, which deals with the depths of the mind. It should never be approached lightly or casually. If reading this book inspires you to try Vipassana, you can contact the addresses listed at the back to find out when and where courses are given.

The purpose here is merely to give an outline of the Vipassana method as it is taught by S. N. Goenka, in the hope that this will widen the understanding of the Buddha's teachings and of the meditation technique that is their essence.

Swimology

Once a young professor was making a sea voyage. He was a highly educated man with a long tail of letters after his name, but he had little experience of life. In the crew of the ship on which he was traveling was an illiterate old sailor. Every evening the sailor would visit the cabin of the young professor to listen to him hold forth on many different subjects. He was very impressed with the learning of the young man.

One evening as the sailor was about to leave the cabin after several hours of conversation, the professor asked, "Old man, have you studied geology?"

"What is that, sir?"

"The science of the earth."

"No sir, I have never been to any school or college. I have never studied anything."

"Old man, you have wasted a quarter of your life."

With a long face the old sailor went away. "If such a learned person says so, certainly it must be true," he thought. "I have wasted a quarter of my life!"

Next evening again as the sailor was about to leave the cabin, the professor asked him, "Old man, have you studied oceanography?"

"What is that, sir?"

"The science of the sea."

"No sir, I have never studied anything."

"Old man, you have wasted half your life."

With a still longer face the sailor went away: "I have wasted half my life; this learned man says so."

Next evening once again the young professor questioned the old sailor: "Old man, have you studied meteorology?"

"What is that, sir? I have never even heard of it."

"Why, the science of the wind, the rain, the weather."

"No sir. As I told you, I have never been to any school. I have never studied anything."

"You have not studied the science of the earth on which you live; you have not studied the science of the sea on which you earn your livelihood; you have not studied the science of the weather which you encounter every day? Old man, you have wasted three quarters of your life."

The old sailor was very unhappy: "This learned man says that I have wasted three quarters of my life! Certainly I must have wasted three quarters of my life."

The next day it was the turn of the old sailor. He came running to the cabin of the young man and cried, "Professor sir, have you studied swimology?"

"Swimology? What do you mean?"

"Can you swim, sir?"

"No, I don't know how to swim."

"Professor sir, you have wasted all your life! The ship has struck a rock and is sinking. Those who can swim may reach the nearby shore, but those who cannot swim will drown. I am so sorry, professor sir, you have surely lost your life."

You may study all the "ologies" of the world, but if you do not learn swimology, all your studies are useless. You may read and write books on swimming, you may debate on its subtle theoretical aspects, but how will that help you if you refuse to enter the water yourself? You must learn how to swim.

Chapter 1

THE SEARCH

All of us seek peace and harmony, because this is what we lack in our lives. We all want to be happy; we regard it as our right. Yet happiness is a goal we strive toward more often than attain. At times we all experience dissatisfaction in life—agitation, irritation, disharmony, suffering. Even if at this moment we are free from such dissatisfactions, we can all remember a time when they afflicted us and can foresee a time when they may recur. Eventually we all must face the suffering of death.

Nor do our personal dissatisfactions remain limited to ourselves; instead, we keep sharing our suffering with others. The atmosphere around each unhappy person becomes charged with agitation, so that all who enter that environment may also feel agitated and unhappy. In this way individual tensions combine to create the tensions of society.

This is the basic problem of life: its unsatisfactory nature. Things happen that we do not want; things that we want do not happen. And we are ignorant of how or why this process works, just as we are each ignorant of our own beginning and end.

Twenty-five centuries ago in northern India, a man decided to investigate this problem, the problem of human suffering. After years of searching and trying various methods, he discovered a way to gain insight into the reality of his own nature and to experience true freedom from suffering. Having reached the highest goal of liberation, of release from misery and conflict, he devoted the rest of his life to helping others do as he had done, showing them the way to liberate themselves.

This person—**Siddhattha Gotama**, known as the Buddha, "the enlightened one"—never claimed to be anything other than a man.

Like all great teachers he became the subject of legends, but no matter what marvelous stories were told of his past existences or his miraculous powers, still all accounts agree that he never claimed to be divine or to be divinely inspired. Whatever special qualities he had were pre-eminently human qualities that he had brought to perfection. Therefore, whatever he achieved is within the grasp of any human being who works as he did.

The Buddha did not teach any religion or philosophy or system of belief. He called his teaching **Dhamma**, that is, "law," the law of nature. He had no interest in dogma or idle speculation. Instead he offered a universal, practical solution for a universal problem. "Now as before," he said, "I teach about suffering and the eradication of suffering."[1] He refused even to discuss anything which did not lead to liberation from misery.

This teaching, he insisted, was not something that he had invented or that was divinely revealed to him. It was simply the truth, reality, which by his own efforts he had succeeded in discovering, as many people before him had done, as many people after him would do. He claimed no monopoly on the truth.

Nor did he assert any special authority for his teaching—neither because of the faith that people had in him, nor because of the apparently logical nature of what he taught. On the contrary, he stated that it is proper to doubt and to test whatever is beyond one's experience:

Do not simply believe whatever you are told, or whatever has been handed down from past generations, or what is common opinion, or whatever the scriptures say. Do not accept something as true merely by deduction or inference, or by considering outward appearances, or by partiality for a certain view, or because of its plausibility, or because your teacher tells you it is so. But when you yourselves directly know, "These principles are unwholesome, blameworthy, condemned by the wise; when adopted and carried out they lead to harm and suffering," then you should abandon them. And when you yourselves directly know, "These principles are wholesome, blameless, praised by the wise; when adopted and carried out they lead to welfare and happiness," then you should accept and practice them.[2]

The highest authority is one's own experience of truth. Nothing should be accepted on faith alone; we have to examine to see whether it is logical, practical, beneficial. Nor having examined a teaching by means of our reason is it sufficient to accept it as true intellectually. If we are to benefit from the truth, we have to experience it directly. Only then can we know that it is really true. The Buddha always emphasized that he taught only what he had experienced by direct knowledge, and he encouraged others to develop such knowledge themselves, to become their own authorities: "Each of you, make yourself an island, make yourself your refuge; there is no other refuge. Make truth your island, make truth your refuge; there is no other refuge."[3]

The only real refuge in life, the only solid ground on which to take a stand, the only authority that can give proper guidance and protection is truth, Dhamma, the law of nature, experienced and verified by oneself. Therefore in his teaching the Buddha always gave highest importance to the direct experience of truth. What he had experienced he explained as clearly as possible so that others might have guidelines with which to work toward their own realization of truth. He said, "The teaching I have presented does not have separate outward and inward versions. Nothing has been kept hidden in the fist of the teacher."[4] He had no esoteric doctrine for a chosen few. On the contrary, he wished to make the law of nature known as plainly and as widely as possible, so that as many people as possible might benefit from it.

Neither was he interested in establishing a sect or a personality cult with himself as its center. The personality of the one who teaches, he maintained, is of minor importance compared to the teaching. His purpose was to show others how to liberate themselves, not to turn them into blind devotees. To a follower who showed excessive veneration for him he said, "What do you gain by seeing this body, which is subject to corruption? He who sees the Dhamma sees me; he who sees me sees the Dhamma."[5]

Devotion toward another person, no matter how saintly, is not sufficient to liberate anyone; there can be no liberation or salvation without direct experience of reality. Therefore truth has primacy, not the one who speaks it. All respect is due to whoever teaches the truth, but the best way to show that respect is by working to realize the truth oneself. When extravagant honors were paid to him near the end of his life, the Buddha commented, "This is not how an enlightened one is properly honored, or shown respect, or revered, or reverenced, or venerated. Rather it is the monk or nun, the lay male or female follower who steadfastly walks on the path of

Dhamma from the first steps to the final goal, who practices Dhamma working in the right way, that honors, respects, reveres, reverences and venerates the enlightened one with the highest respect."[6]

What the Buddha taught was a way that each human being can follow. He called this path the Noble Eightfold Path, meaning a practice of eight interrelated parts. It is noble in the sense that anyone who walks on the path is bound to become a noble-hearted, saintly person, freed from suffering.

It is a path of insight into the nature of reality, a path of truth-realization. In order to solve our problems, we have to see our situation as it really is. We must learn to recognize superficial, apparent reality, and also to penetrate beyond appearances so as to perceive subtler truths, then ultimate truth, and finally to experience the truth of freedom from suffering. Whatever name we choose to give this truth of liberation, whether **nibbāna**, "heaven," or anything else, is unimportant. The important thing is to experience it.

The only way to experience truth directly is to look within, to observe oneself. All our lives we have been accustomed to look outward. We have always been interested in what is happening outside, what others are doing. We have rarely if ever tried to examine ourselves, our own mental and physical structure, our own actions, our own reality. Therefore we remain unknown to ourselves. We do not realize how harmful this ignorance is, how much we remain the slaves of forces within ourselves of which we are unaware.

This inner darkness must be dispelled to apprehend the truth. We must gain insight into our own nature in order to understand the nature of existence. Therefore the path that the Buddha showed is a path of introspection, of self-observation. He said, "Within this very fathom-long body containing the mind with its perceptions, I make known the universe, its origin, its cessation, and the way leading to its cessation."[7] The entire universe and the laws of nature by which it works are to be experienced within oneself. They can *only* be experienced within oneself.

The path is also a path of purification. We investigate the truth about ourselves not out of idle intellectual curiosity but rather with a definite purpose. By observing ourselves we become aware for the first time of the conditioned reactions, the prejudices that cloud our mental vision, that hide reality from us and produce suffering.

We recognize the accumulated inner tensions that keep us agitated, miserable, and we realize they can be removed. Gradually we learn how to allow them to dissolve, and our minds become pure, peaceful, and happy.

The path is a process requiring continual application. Sudden breakthroughs may come, but they are the result of sustained efforts. It is necessary to work step by step; with every step, however, the benefits are immediate. We do not follow the path in the hope of accruing benefits to be enjoyed only in the future, of attaining after death a heaven that is known here only by conjecture. The benefits must be concrete, vivid, personal, experienced here and now.

Above all, it is a teaching to be practiced. Simply having faith in the Buddha or his teachings will not help to free us from suffering; neither will a merely intellectual understanding of the path. Both of these are of value only if they inspire us to put the teachings into practice. Only the actual practice of what the Buddha taught will give concrete results and change our lives for the better. The Buddha said,

Someone may recite much of the texts, but if he does not practice them, such a heedless person is like a herdsman who only counts the cows of others: he does not enjoy the rewards of the life of a truth-seeker.

Another may be able to recite only a few words from the texts, but if he lives the life of Dhamma, taking steps on the path from its beginning to the goal, then he enjoys the rewards of the life of a truth-seeker.[8]

The path must be followed, the teaching must be implemented; otherwise it is a meaningless exercise.

It is not necessary to call oneself a Buddhist in order to practice this teaching. Labels are irrelevant. Suffering makes no distinctions, but is common to all; therefore the remedy, to be useful, must be equally applicable to all. Neither is the practice reserved only for recluses who are divorced from ordinary life. Certainly a period must be given in which to devote oneself exclusively to the task of learning how to practice, but having done so one must apply the teaching in daily life. Someone who forsakes home and worldly responsibilities in order to follow the path has the opportunity to work more intensively, to assimilate the teaching more deeply, and therefore to progress more quickly. On the other hand, someone involved in worldly life, juggling the claims of many different responsibilities, can give only limited time to the practice. But whether homeless or householder, one must apply Dhamma.

It is only applied Dhamma that gives results. If this is truly a way from suffering to peace, then as we progress in the practice we should become more happy in our daily lives, more harmonious, more at peace with ourselves. At the same time our relations with others should become more peaceful and harmonious. Instead of adding to the tensions of society, we should be able to make a positive contribution that will increase the happiness and welfare of all. To follow the path we must live the life of Dhamma, of truth, of purity. This is the proper way to implement the teaching. Dhamma, practiced correctly, is the art of living.

Questions and Answers

QUESTION: *You keep referring to the Buddha. Are you teaching Buddhism?*

S. N. GOENKA: I am not concerned with "isms." I teach Dhamma, that is, what the Buddha taught. He never taught any "ism" or sectarian doctrine. He taught something from which people of every background can benefit: an art of living. Remaining in ignorance is harmful for everyone; developing wisdom is good for everyone. So anyone can practice this technique and find benefit. A Christian will become a good Christian, a Jew will become a good Jew, a Muslim will become a good Muslim, a Hindu will become a good Hindu, a Buddhist will become a good Buddhist. One must become a good human being; otherwise one can never be a good Christian, a good Jew, a good Muslim, a good Hindu, a good Buddhist. How to become a good human being—that is most important.

You talk about conditioning. Isn't this training really a kind of conditioning of the mind, even if a positive one?

On the contrary, it is a process of de-conditioning. Instead of imposing anything on the mind, it automatically removes unwholesome qualities so that only wholesome, positive ones remain. By eliminating negativities, it uncovers the positivity which is the basic nature of a pure mind.

But over a period of time, to sit in a particular posture and direct the attention in a certain way is a form of conditioning.

If you do it as a game or mechanical ritual, then yes—you condition the mind. But that is a misuse of Vipassana. When it is practiced correctly, it enables you to experience truth directly, for yourself. And from this experience, naturally understanding develops, which destroys all previous conditioning.

Isn't it selfish to forget about the world and just to sit and meditate all day?

It would be if this were an end in itself, but it is a means to an end that is not at all selfish: a healthy mind. When your body is sick, you enter a hospital to recover health. You don't go there for your whole life, but simply to regain health, which you will then use in ordinary life. In the same way you come to a meditation course to gain mental health, which you will then use in ordinary life for your good and for the good of others.

To remain happy and peaceful even when confronted by the suffering of others—isn't that sheer insensitivity?

Being sensitive to the suffering of others does not mean that you must become sad yourself. Instead you should remain calm and balanced, so that you can act to alleviate their suffering. If you also become sad, you increase the unhappiness around you; you do not help others, you do not help yourself.

Why don't we live in a state of peace?

Because wisdom is lacking. A life without wisdom is a life of illusion, which is a state of agitation, of misery. Our first responsibility is to live a healthy, harmonious life, good for ourselves and for all others. To do so, we must learn to use our faculty of self-observation, truth-observation.

Why is it necessary to join a ten-day course to learn the technique?

Well, if you could come for longer that would be better still! But ten days is the minimum time in which it is possible to grasp the outlines of the technique.

Why must we remain within the course site for the ten days?

Because you are here to perform an operation on your mind. An operation must be done in a hospital, in an operating theater protected from contamination. Here within the boundaries of the course, you can perform the operation without being disturbed by any outside influence. When the course is over the operation has ended, and you are ready once again to face the world.

Does this technique heal the physical body?

Yes, as a by-product. Many psychosomatic diseases naturally disappear when mental tensions are dissolved. If the mind is agitated, physical diseases are bound to develop. When the mind becomes calm and pure, automatically they will go away. But if you take the curing of a physical disease as your goal instead of the purification of your mind, you achieve neither one nor the other. I have found that people who join a course with the aim of curing a physical illness have their attention fixed only on their disease throughout the course: "Today, is it better? No, not better. . . . Today, is it improving? No, not improving!" All the ten days they waste in this way. But if the intention is simply to purify the mind, then many diseases automatically go away as a result of meditation.

What would you say is the purpose of life?

To come out of misery. A human being has the wonderful ability to go deep inside, observe reality, and come out of suffering. Not to use this ability is to waste one's life. Use it to live a really healthy, happy life!

You speak of being overpowered by negativity. How about being overpowered by positivity, for example, by love?

What you call "positivity" is the real nature of the mind. When the mind is free of conditioning, it is always full of love—pure love—and you feel peaceful and happy. If you remove the negativity, then positivity remains, purity remains. Let the entire world be overwhelmed by this positivity!

To Walk on the Path

In the city of Sāvatthi in northern India, the Buddha had a large center where people would come to meditate and to listen to his Dhamma talks. Every evening one young man used to come to hear his discourses. For years he came to listen to the Buddha but never put any of the teaching into practice.

After a few years, one evening this man came a little early and found the Buddha alone. He approached him and said, "Sir, I have a question that keeps arising in my mind, raising doubts."

"Oh? There should not be any doubts on the path of Dhamma; have them clarified. What is your question?"

"Sir, for many years now I have been coming to your meditation center, and I have noticed that there are a large number of recluses around you, monks and nuns, and a still larger number of lay people, both men and women. For years some of them have been coming to you. Some of them, I can see, have certainly reached the final stage; quite obviously they are fully liberated. I can also see that others have experienced some change in their lives. They are better than they were before, although I cannot say that they are fully liberated. But sir, I also notice that a large number of people, including myself, are as they were, or sometimes they are even worse. They have not changed at all, or have not changed for the better.

"Why should this be, sir? People come to you, such a great man, fully enlightened, such a powerful, compassionate person. Why don't you use your power and compassion to liberate them all?"

The Buddha smiled and said, "Young man, where do you live? What is your native place?"

"Sir, I live here in Sāvatthi, this capital city of the state of Kosala."

"Yes, but your facial features show that you are not from this part of the country. Where are you from originally?"

"Sir, I am from the city of Rājagaha, the capital of the state of Magadha. I came and settled here in Sāvatthi a few years ago."

"And have you severed all connections with Rājagaha?"

"No sir. I still have relatives there. I have friends there. I have business there."

"Then certainly you must go from Sāvatthi to Rājagaha quite often?"

"Yes sir. Many times each year I visit Rājagaha and return to Sāvatthi."

"Having traveled and returned so many times on the path from here to Rājagaha, certainly you must know the path very well?"

"Oh yes sir, I know it perfectly. I might almost say that even if I was blindfolded I could find the path to Rājagaha, so many times have I walked it."

"And your friends, those who know you well, certainly they must know that you are from Rājagaha and have settled here? They must know that you often visit Rājagaha and return, and that you know the path from here to Rājagaha perfectly?"

"Oh yes, sir. All those who are close to me know that I often go to Rājagaha and that I know the path perfectly."

"Then it must happen that some of them come to you and ask you to explain to them the path from here to Rājagaha. Do you hide anything or do you explain the path to them clearly?"

"What is there to hide, sir? I explain it to them as clearly as I can: you start walking toward the east and then head toward Banaras, and continue onward until you reach Gaya and then Rājagaha. I explain it very plainly to them, sir."

"And these people to whom you give such clear explanation, do all of them reach Rājagaha?"

"How can that be, sir? Those who walk the entire path to its end, only they will reach Rājagaha."

"This is what I want to explain to you, young man. People keep coming to me knowing that this is someone who has walked the path from here to *nibbāna* and so knows it perfectly. They come to me and ask, 'What is the path to *nibbāna*, to liberation?' And what is there to hide? I explain it to them clearly: 'This is the path.' If somebody just nods his head and says, 'Well said, well said, a very good path, but I won't take a step on it; a wonderful path, but I won't take the trouble to walk over it,' then how can such a person reach the final goal?

"I do not carry anyone on my shoulders to take him to the final goal. *Nobody* can carry anyone else on his shoulders to the final goal. At most, with love and compassion one can say, 'Well, this is the path, and this is how I have walked on it. You also work, you also walk, and you will reach the final goal.' But each person has to walk himself, has to take every step on the path himself. He who has taken one step on the path is one step nearer the goal. He who has taken a hundred steps is a hundred steps nearer the goal. He who has taken all the steps on the path has reached the final goal. You have to walk on the path yourself."⁹

Chapter 2

THE STARTING POINT

The source of suffering lies within each of us. When we understand our own reality, we shall recognize the solution to the problem of suffering. "Know thyself," all wise persons have advised. We must begin by knowing our own nature; otherwise we can never solve our own problems or the problems of the world.

But actually what do we know about ourselves? We are each convinced of the importance of ourselves, of the uniqueness of ourselves, but our knowledge of ourselves is only superficial. At deeper levels, we do not know ourselves at all.

The Buddha examined the phenomenon of a human being by examining his own nature. Laying aside all preconceptions, he explored reality within and realized that every being is a composite of five processes, four of them mental and one physical.

Matter

Let us begin with the physical aspect. This is the most obvious, the most apparent portion of ourselves, readily perceived by all the senses. And yet how little we really know about it. Superficially one can control the body: it moves and acts according to the conscious will. But on another level, all the internal organs function beyond our control, without our knowledge. At a subtler level, we know nothing, experientially, of the incessant biochemical reactions occurring within each cell of the body. But this is still not the ultimate reality of the material phenomenon. Ultimately the seemingly solid body is composed of subatomic particles and empty space. What is more, even these subatomic particles have no real solidity; the existence span of one of them is much less than a trillionth of a second. Particles continuously arise and vanish, passing into and out of existence, like a flow of vibrations. This is the ultimate reality of the body, of all matter, discovered by the Buddha 2500 years ago.

Through their own investigations, modern scientists have recognized and accepted this ultimate reality of the material universe. However, these scientists have not become liberated, enlightened persons. Out of curiosity they have investigated the nature of the universe, using their intellects and relying on instruments to verify their theories. In contrast, the Buddha was motivated not simply by curiosity but rather by the wish to find a way out of suffering. He used no instrument in his investigation other than his own mind. The truth that he discovered was the result not of intellectualizing but of his own direct experience, and that is why it could liberate him.

He found that the entire material universe was composed of particles, called in Pāli **kalāpas**, or "indivisible units." These units exhibit in endless variation the basic qualities of matter: mass, cohesion, temperature, and movement. They combine to form structures which seem to have some permanence. But actually these are all composed of minuscule *kalāpas* which are in a state of continuously arising and passing away. This is the ultimate reality of matter: a constant stream of waves or particles. This is the body which we each call "myself."

Mind

Along with the physical process there is the psychic process, the mind. Although it cannot be touched or seen, it seems even more intimately connected with ourselves than our bodies: we may picture a future existence without the body, but we cannot imagine any such existence without the mind. Yet how little we know about the mind, and how little we are able to control it. How often it refuses to do what we want, and does what we do not want. Our control of the conscious mind is tenuous enough, but the unconscious seems totally beyond our power or understanding, filled with forces of which we may not approve or be aware.

As he examined the body, the Buddha also examined the mind and found that in broad, overall terms it consisted of four processes: consciousness (**viññāṇa**), perception (**saññā**), sensation (**vedanā**), and reaction (**sankhāra**).

The first process, consciousness, is the receiving part of the mind, the act of undifferentiated awareness or cognition. It simply registers the occurrence of any phenomenon, the reception of any input, physical or mental. It notes the raw data of experience without assigning labels or making value judgments.

The second mental process is perception, the act of recognition. This part of the mind identifies whatever has been noted by the consciousness. It distinguishes, labels, and categorizes the incoming raw data and makes evaluations, positive or negative.

The next part of the mind is sensation. Actually as soon as any input is received, sensation arises, a signal that something is happening. So long as the input is not evaluated, the sensation remains neutral. But once a value is attached to the incoming data, the sensation becomes pleasant or unpleasant, depending on the evaluation given.

If the sensation is pleasant, a wish forms to prolong and intensify the experience. If it is an unpleasant sensation, the wish is to stop it, to push it away. The mind reacts with liking or disliking.[1] For example, when the ear is functioning normally and one hears a sound, cognition is at work. When the sound is recognized as words, with positive or negative connotations, perception has started to function. Next sensation comes into play. If the words are praise, a pleasant sensation arises. If they are abuse, an unpleasant sensation arises. At once reaction takes place. If the sensation is pleasant, one starts liking it, wanting more words of praise. If the sensation is unpleasant, one starts disliking it, wanting to stop the abuse.

The same steps occur whenever any of the other senses receives an input: consciousness, perception, sensation, reaction. These four mental functions are even more fleeting than the ephemeral particles composing the material reality. Each moment that the senses come into contact with any object, the four mental processes occur with lightning-like rapidity and repeat themselves with each subsequent moment of contact. So rapidly does this occur, however, that one is unaware of what is happening. It is only when a particular reaction has been repeated over a longer period of time and has taken a pronounced, intensified form that awareness of it develops at the conscious level.

The most striking aspect of this description of a human being is not what it includes but what it omits. Whether we are Western or Eastern, whether Christian, Jewish, Muslim, Hindu, Buddhist, atheist, or anything else, each of us has a congenital assurance that there is an "I" somewhere within us, a continuing identity. We operate on the unthinking assumption that the person who existed ten years ago is essentially the same person who exists today, who will exist ten years from now, perhaps who will still exist in a future life after death. No matter what philosophies or theories or beliefs we hold as true, actually we each live our lives with the deep-rooted conviction, "I was, I am, I shall be."

The Buddha challenged this instinctive assertion of identity. By doing so he was not expounding one more speculative view to combat the theories of others: he repeatedly emphasized that he was not putting forth an opinion, but simply describing the truth that he had experienced and that any ordinary person can experience. "The enlightened one has cast aside all theories," he said, "for he has seen the reality of matter, sensation, perception, reaction, and consciousness, and their arising and passing away."[2] Despite appearances, he had found that each human being is in fact a series of separate but related events. Each event is the result of the preceding one and follows it without any interval. The unbroken progression of closely connected events gives the appearance of continuity, of identity, but this is only an apparent reality, not ultimate truth.

We may give a river a name but actually it is a flow of water never pausing in its course. We may think of the light of a candle as something constant, but if we look closely, we see that it is really a flame arising from a wick which burns for a moment, to be replaced at once by a new flame, moment after moment. We talk of the light of an electric lamp, never pausing to think that in reality it is, like the river, a constant flow, in this case a flow of energy caused by very high frequency oscillations taking place within the filament. Every moment something new arises as a product of the past, to be replaced by something new in the following moment. The succession of events is so rapid and continuous that it is difficult to discern. At a particular point in the process one cannot say that what occurs now is the same as what preceded it, nor can one say that it is not the same. Nevertheless, the process occurs.

In the same way, the Buddha realized, a person is not a finished, unchanging entity but a process flowing from moment to moment. There is no real "being," merely an ongoing flow, a continuous process of becoming. Of course in daily life we must deal with each other as persons of more or less defined, unchanging nature; we must accept external, apparent reality, or else we could not function at all. External reality is a reality, but only a superficial one. At a deeper level the reality is that the entire universe, animate and inanimate, is in a constant state of becoming—of arising and passing away. Each of us is in fact a stream of constantly changing subatomic particles, along with which the processes of consciousness, perception, sensation, reaction change even more rapidly than the physical process.

This is the ultimate reality of the self with which each of us is so concerned. This is the course of events in which we are involved. If we can understand it properly by direct experience, we shall find the clue to lead us out of suffering.

Questions and Answers

QUESTION: *When you say "mind," I'm not sure what you mean. I can't find the mind.*

S. N. GOENKA: It is everywhere, with every atom. Wherever you feel anything, the mind is there. The mind feels.

Then by the mind you don't mean the brain?

Oh no, no, no. Here in the West you think that the mind is only in the head. It is a wrong notion.

Mind is in the whole body?

Yes, the whole body contains the mind, the whole body!

You speak of the experience of "I" only in negative terms. Hasn't it a positive side? Isn't there an experience of "I" which fills a person with joy, peace, and rapture?

By meditation you will find that all such sensual pleasures are impermanent; they come and pass away. If this "I" really enjoys them, if they are "my" pleasures, then "I" must have some mastery over them. But they just arise and pass away without my control. What "I" is there?

I'm speaking not of sensual pleasures but of a very deep level.

At that level, "I" is of no importance at all. When you reach that level, the ego is dissolved. There is only joy. The question of "I" does not arise then.

Well, instead of "I," let us say the experience of a person.

Feeling feels; there is no one to feel it. Things are just happening, that's all. Now it seems to you that there must be an "I" who feels, but if you practice, you will reach the stage where ego dissolves. Then your question will disappear!

I came here because I felt "I" needed to come here.

Yes! Quite true. For conventional purposes, we cannot run away from "I" or "mine." But clinging to them, taking them as real in an ultimate sense will bring only suffering.

I was wondering whether there are people who cause suffering for us?

Nobody causes suffering for you. You cause the suffering for yourself by generating tensions in the mind. If you know how not to do that, it becomes easy to remain peaceful and happy in every situation.

What about when someone else is doing wrong to us?

You must not allow people to do wrong to you. Whenever someone does something wrong, he harms others and at the same time he harms himself. If you allow him to do wrong, you are encouraging him to do wrong. You must use all your strength to stop him, but with only good will, compassion, and sympathy for that person. If you act with hatred or anger, then you aggravate the situation. But you cannot have good will for such a person unless your mind is calm and peaceful. So practice to develop peace within yourself, and then you can solve the problem.

What is the point of seeking peace within when there is no peace in the world?

The world will be peaceful only when the people of the world are peaceful and happy. The change has to begin with each individual. If the jungle is withered and you want to restore it to life, you must water each tree of that jungle. If you want world peace, you ought to learn how to be peaceful yourself. Only then can you bring peace to the world.

I can understand how meditation will help maladjusted, unhappy people, but how about someone who feels satisfied with his life, who is already happy?

Someone who remains satisfied with the superficial pleasures of life is ignorant of the agitation deep within the mind. He is under the illusion that he is a happy person, but his pleasures are not lasting, and the tensions generated in the unconscious keep increasing, to appear sooner or later at the conscious level of the mind. When they do, this so-called happy person becomes miserable. So why not start working here and now to avert that situation?

Is your teaching Mahāyāna or Hīnayāna?

Neither. The word *yāna* actually means a vehicle that will carry you to the final goal, but today it is mistakenly given a sectarian connotation. The Buddha never taught anything sectarian. He taught Dhamma, which is universal. This universality is what attracted me to the teachings of the Buddha, which gave me benefit, and therefore this universal Dhamma is what I offer to one and all, with all my love and compassion. For me, Dhamma is neither *Mahāyāna,* nor *Hīnayāna,* nor any sect.

The Buddha and the Scientist

The physical reality is changing constantly every moment. This is what the Buddha realized by examining himself. With his strongly concentrated mind, he penetrated deeply into his own nature and found that the entire material structure is composed of minute subatomic particles which are continuously arising and vanishing. In the snapping of a finger or the blinking of an eye, he said, each one of these particles arises and passes away many trillions of times.

"Unbelievable," anyone will think who observes only the apparent reality of the body, which seems so solid, so permanent. I used to suppose that the phrase "many trillions of times" might be an idiomatic expression not to be taken literally. However, modern science has confirmed this statement.

Several years ago, an American scientist received the Nobel Prize in physics. For a long time he had studied and conducted experiments to learn about the subatomic particles of which the physical universe is composed. It was already known that these particles arise and pass away with great rapidity, over and over again. Now this scientist decided to develop an instrument that would be able to count how many times a particle arises and passes away in one second. He very rightly called the instrument that he invented a bubble chamber, and he found that in one second a subatomic particle arises and vanishes 10^{22} times.

The truth that this scientist discovered is the same as that which the Buddha found, but what a great difference between them! Some of my American students who had taken courses in India later returned to their country, and they visited this scientist. They reported to me that despite the fact that he has discovered this reality, he is still an ordinary person with the usual stock of misery that all ordinary people have! He is not totally liberated from suffering.

No, that scientist has not become an enlightened person, not been freed from all suffering, because he has not experienced truth directly. What he has learned is still only intellectual wisdom. He believes this truth because he has faith in the instrument which he has invented, but he has not *experienced* the truth himself.

I have nothing against this man nor against modern science. However, one must not be a scientist only of the world outside. Like the Buddha, one should also be a scientist of the world within, in order to experience truth directly. Personal realization of truth will automatically change the habit pattern of the mind so that one starts to live according to the truth. Every action becomes directed toward one's own good and the good of others. If this inner experience is missing, science is liable to be misused for destructive ends. But if we become scientists of the reality within, we shall make proper use of science for the happiness of all.

Chapter 3

THE IMMEDIATE CAUSE

The real world bears no resemblance to the world of fairytales in which everyone lives happily ever after. We cannot avoid the truth that life is imperfect, incomplete, unsatisfactory—the truth of the existence of suffering.

Given this reality, the important things for us to know are whether suffering has a cause, and, if so, whether it is possible to remove that cause, so that suffering may be removed. If the events that cause our suffering are simply random occurrences over which we can have no control or influence, then we are powerless and might as well give up the attempt to find a way out of suffering. Or if our sufferings are dictated by an omnipotent being acting in an arbitrary and inscrutable manner, then we ought to find out how to propitiate this being so that he will no longer inflict suffering on us.

The Buddha realized that our suffering is not merely a product of chance. There are causes behind it, as there are causes for all phenomena. The law of cause and effect—**kamma**—is universal and fundamental to existence. Nor are the causes beyond our control.

Kamma

The word *kamma* (or, in its more widely known Sanskrit form, *karma*) is popularly understood as meaning "fate." Unfortunately, the connotations of this word are exactly opposite to what the Buddha intended by *kamma*. Fate is something outside our control, the decree of providence, what has been preordained for each one of us. *Kamma,* however, literally means "action." Our own actions are the causes of whatever we experience: "All beings own their deeds, inherit their deeds, originate from their deeds, are tied to their deeds; their deeds are their refuge. As their deeds are base or noble, so will be their lives."[1]

Everything that we encounter in life is the result of our own actions. Consequently, we can each become master of our fate by becoming master of our actions. Each of us is responsible for the actions that give rise to our suffering. Each of us has the means to end the suffering in our actions. The Buddha said,

> You are your own master,
> You make your own future.[2]

As it is, each of us is like a blindfolded man who has never learned to drive, sitting behind the wheel of a speeding car on a busy highway. He is not likely to reach his destination without mishap. He may think that he is driving the car, but actually the car is driving him. If he wants to avoid an accident, let alone arrive at his goal, he should remove the blindfold, learn how to operate the vehicle, and steer it out of danger as quickly as possible. Similarly, we must become aware of what we do and then learn to perform actions that will lead us where we really wish to go.

Three Types of Actions

There are three types of actions: physical, vocal, and mental. Normally we attach most importance to physical actions, less to vocal actions, and least to mental actions. Beating a person appears to us a graver action than speaking to him insultingly, and both seem more serious than an unexpressed ill will toward the person. Certainly this would be the view according to the man-made laws of each country. But according to Dhamma, the law of nature, mental action is most important. A physical or vocal action assumes totally different significance according to the intention with which it is done.

A surgeon uses his scalpel to perform an emergency life-saving operation which turns out to be unsuccessful, leading to the death of the patient; a murderer uses his dagger to stab his victim to death. Physically their actions are similar, with the same effect, but mentally they are poles apart. The surgeon acts out of compassion, the murderer out of hatred. The result each achieves will be totally different, according to his mental action.

Similarly, in the case of speech, the intention is most important. A man quarrels with a colleague and abuses him, calling him a fool. He speaks out of anger. The same man sees his child playing in the mud and tenderly calls him a fool. He speaks out of love. In both cases the same words are spoken, but to express virtually opposite states of mind. It is the intention of our speech which determines the result.

Words and deeds or their external effects are merely consequences of mental action. They are properly judged according to the nature of the intention to which they give expression. It is the mental action which is the real *kamma*, the cause which will give results in future. Understanding this truth the Buddha announced,

> Mind precedes all phenomena,
> mind matters most, everything is mind-made.
> If with an impure mind
> you speak or act,
> then suffering follows you
> as the cartwheel follows the foot of the draft animal.

> If with a pure mind
> you speak or act,
> then happiness follows you
> as a shadow that never departs.[3]

The Cause of Suffering

But which mental actions determine our fate? If the mind consists of nothing but consciousness, perception, sensation, and reaction, then which of these gives rise to suffering? Each of them is involved to some degree in the process of suffering. However, the first three are primarily passive. Consciousness merely receives the raw data of experience, perception places the data in a category, sensation signals the occurring of the previous steps. The job of these three is only to digest incoming information. But when the mind starts to react, passivity gives way to attraction or repulsion, liking or disliking. This reaction sets in motion a fresh chain of events. At the beginning of the chain is reaction, *sankhāra*. This is why the Buddha said,

Whatever suffering arises
has a reaction as its cause.
If all reactions cease to be
then there is no more suffering.[4]

The real *kamma,* the real cause of suffering is the reaction of the mind. One fleeting reaction of liking or disliking may not be very strong and may not give much result, but it can have a cumulative effect. The reaction is repeated moment after moment, intensifying with each repetition, and developing into craving or aversion. This is what in his first sermon the Buddha called **taṇhā**, literally "thirst": the mental habit of insatiable longing for what is not, which implies an equal and irremediable dissatisfaction with what is.[5] And the stronger longing and dissatisfaction become, the deeper their influence on our thinking, our speech, and our actions—and the more suffering they will cause.

Some reactions, the Buddha said, are like lines drawn on the surface of a pool of water: as soon as they are drawn they are erased. Others are like lines traced on a sandy beach: if drawn in the morning they are gone by night, wiped away by the tide or the wind. Others are like lines cut deeply into rock with chisel and hammer. They too will be obliterated as the rock erodes, but it will take ages for them to disappear.[6]

Throughout each day of our lives the mind keeps generating reactions, but if at the end of the day we try to remember them, we shall be able to recall only one or two which made a deep impression that day. Again, if at the end of a month we try to remember all our reactions, we shall be able to recall only one or two which made the deepest impression that month. Again, at the end of a year we shall be able to recall only the one or two reactions that left the deepest impression during that year. Such deep reactions as these are very dangerous and lead to immense suffering.

The first step toward emerging from such suffering is to accept the reality of it, not as a philosophical concept or an article of faith, but as a fact of existence which affects each one of us in our lives. With this acceptance and an understanding of what suffering is and why we suffer, we can stop being driven and start to drive. By learning to realize directly our own nature, we can set ourselves on the path leading out of suffering.

Questions and Answers

QUESTION: *Isn't suffering a natural part of life? Why should we try to escape from it?*

S. N. GOENKA: We have become so involved in suffering that to be free from it seems unnatural. But when you experience the real happiness of mental purity, you will know that this is the natural state of the mind.

Can't the experience of suffering ennoble people and help them to grow in character?

Yes. In fact, this technique deliberately uses suffering as a tool to make one a noble person. But it will work only if you learn how to observe suffering objectively. If you are attached to your suffering, the experience will not ennoble you; you will always remain miserable.

Isn't taking control of our actions a kind of suppression?

No. You learn just to observe objectively whatever is happening. If someone is angry and tries to hide his anger, to swallow it, then, yes, it's suppression. But by observing the anger, you will find that automatically it passes away. You become free from the anger if you learn how to observe it objectively.

If we keep observing ourselves, how can we live life in any natural way? We'll be so busy watching ourselves that we can't act freely or spontaneously.

That is not what people find after completing a meditation course. Here you learn a mental training that will give you the ability to observe yourself in daily life whenever you need to do so. Not that you will keep practicing with closed eyes all day throughout your life, but just as the strength you gain by physical exercise helps you in daily life, so this mental exercise will also strengthen you. What you call "free, spontaneous action" is really blind reaction, which is always harmful. By learning to observe yourself, you will find that whenever a difficult situation arises in life, you can keep the balance of your mind. With that balance you can choose freely how to act. You will take real action, which is always positive, always beneficial for you and for all others.

Aren't there any chance happenings, random occurrences without a cause?

Nothing happens without a cause. It is not possible. Sometimes our limited senses and intellects cannot clearly find it, but that does not mean that there is no cause.

Are you saying that everything in life is predetermined?

Well, certainly our past actions will give fruit, good or bad. They will determine the type of life we have, the general situation in which we find ourselves. But that does not mean that whatever happens to us is predestined, ordained by our past actions, and that nothing else can happen. This is not the case. Our past actions influence the flow of our lives, directing them toward pleasant or unpleasant experiences. But present actions are equally important. Nature has given us the ability to become masters of our present actions. With that mastery we can change our future.

But surely the actions of others also affect us?

Of course. We are influenced by the people around us and by our environment, and we keep influencing them as well. If the majority of people, for example, are in favor of violence, then war and destruction occur, causing many to suffer. But if people start to purify their minds, then violence cannot happen. The root of the problem lies in the mind of each individual human being, because society is composed of individuals. If each person starts changing, then society will change, and war and destruction will become rare events.

How can we help each other if each person must face the results of his own actions?

Our own mental actions have an influence on others. If we generate nothing but negativity in the mind, that negativity has a harmful effect on those who come into contact with us. If we fill the mind with positivity, with good will toward others, then it will have a helpful effect on those around us. You cannot control the actions, the *kamma* of others, but you can become master of yourself in order to have a positive influence on those around you.

Why is being wealthy good karma? If it is, does that mean to say that most people in the West have good karma and most people in the Third World have bad karma?

Wealth alone is not a good karma. If you become wealthy but remain miserable, what is the use of this wealth? Having wealth and also happiness, real happiness—that is good karma. Most important is to be happy, whether you are wealthy or not.

Surely it is unnatural never to react?

It seems so if you have experienced only the wrong habit-pattern of an impure mind. But it is natural for a pure mind to remain detached, full of love, compassion, good will, joy, equanimity. Learn to experience that.

How can we be involved in life unless we react?

Instead of reacting you learn to act, to act with a balanced mind. Vipassana meditators do not become inactive, like vegetables. They learn how to act positively. If you can change your life pattern from reaction to action, then you have attained something very valuable. And you can change it by practicing Vipassana.

Seed and Fruit

As the cause is, so the effect will be. As the seed is, so the fruit will be. As the action is, so the result will be.

In the same soil a farmer plants two seeds: one a seed of sugar cane, the other a seed of a *neem* tree, a tropical tree which is very bitter. Two seeds in the same earth, receiving the same water, the same sunshine, the same air; nature gives the same nourishment to both. Two tiny plants emerge and start growing. And what has happened to the *neem* tree? It has developed with bitterness in every fiber, while the sugar cane has developed with every fiber of it sweet. Why is nature, or, if you prefer, why is God so kind to one and so cruel to the other?

No, no, nature is neither kind nor cruel. It works according to fixed laws. Nature only helps the quality of the seed to manifest. All the nourishment merely helps the seed to reveal the quality that is latent within itself. The seed of the sugar cane has the quality of sweetness; therefore the plant will have nothing but sweetness. The seed of the *neem* tree has the quality of bitterness; the plant will have nothing but bitterness. As the seed is, so the fruit will be.

The farmer goes to the *neem* tree, bows down three times, walks around it 108 times, and then offers flowers, incense, candles, fruit, and sweets. And then he starts praying, "Oh *neem* god, please give me sweet mangoes, I want sweet mangoes!" Poor *neem* god, he cannot give them, he has no power to do so. If someone wants sweet mangoes, he ought to plant a seed of a mango tree. Then he need not cry and beg for help from anyone. The fruit that he will get will be nothing but sweet mangoes. As the seed is, so the fruit will be.

Our difficulty, our ignorance is that we remain unheedful while planting seeds. We keep planting seeds of *neem,* but when the time comes for fruit we are suddenly alert, we want sweet mangoes. And we keep crying and praying and hoping for mangoes. This doesn't work.[7]

Chapter 4

THE ROOT OF THE PROBLEM

"The truth of suffering," the Buddha said, "must be explored to its end."[1] On the night that he was to attain enlightenment, he sat down with the determination not to rise until he had understood how suffering originates and how it can be eradicated.

Suffering Defined

Clearly, he saw, suffering exists. This is an inescapable fact, no matter how unpalatable it may be. Suffering begins with the beginning of life. We have no conscious recollection of existence within the confines of the womb, but the common experience is that we emerge from it crying. Birth is a great trauma.

Having started life, we are all bound to encounter the sufferings of sickness and old age. Yet no matter how sick we may be, no matter how decayed and decrepit, none of us wants to die, because death is a great misery.

Every living creature must face all these sufferings. And as we pass through life, we are bound to encounter other sufferings, various types of physical or mental pain. We become involved with the unpleasant and separated from the pleasant. We fail to get what we want; instead we get what we do not want. All these situations are suffering.

These instances of suffering are readily apparent to anyone who thinks about it deeply. But the future Buddha was not to be satisfied with the limited explanations of the intellect. He continued probing within himself to experience the real nature of suffering, and he found that "attachment to the five aggregates is suffering."[2] At a very deep level, suffering is the inordinate attachment that each one of us has developed toward this body and toward this mind, with its cognitions, perceptions, sensations, and reactions. People cling strongly to their identity—their mental and physical being—when actually there are only evolving processes. This clinging to an unreal idea of oneself, to something that in fact is constantly changing, is suffering.

Attachment

There are several types of attachment. First there is the attachment to the habit of seeking sensual gratification. An addict takes a drug because he wishes to experience the pleasurable sensation that the drug produces in him, even though he knows that by taking the drug he reinforces his addiction. In the same way we are addicted to the condition of craving. As soon as one desire is satisfied, we generate another. The object is secondary; the fact is that we seek to maintain the state of craving continually, because this very craving produces in us a pleasurable sensation that we wish to prolong. Craving becomes a habit that we cannot break, an addiction. And just as an addict gradually develops tolerance toward his chosen drug and requires ever larger doses in order to achieve intoxication, our cravings steadily become stronger the more we seek to fulfill them. In this way we can never come to the end of craving. And so long as we crave, we can never be happy.

Another great attachment is to the "I," the ego, the image we have of ourselves. For each of us, the "I" is the most important person in the world. We behave like a magnet surrounded by iron filings: it will automatically arrange the filings in a pattern centered on itself, and with just as little reflection we all instinctively try to arrange the world according to our liking, seeking to attract the pleasant and to repel the unpleasant. But none of us is alone in the world; one "I" is bound to come into conflict with another. The pattern each seeks to create is disturbed by the magnetic fields of others, and we ourselves become subject to attraction or repulsion. The result can only be unhappiness, suffering.

Nor do we limit attachment to the "I": we extend it to "mine," whatever belongs to us. We each develop great attachment to what we possess, because it is associated with us, it supports the image of "I." This attachment would cause no problem if what one called "mine" were eternal, and the "I" remained to enjoy it eternally. But the fact is that sooner or later the "I" is separated from the "mine." The parting time is bound to come. When it arrives, the greater the clinging to "mine," the greater the suffering will be.

And attachment extends still further—to our views and our beliefs. No matter what their actual content may be, no matter whether they are right or wrong, if we are attached to them they will certainly make us unhappy. We are each convinced that our own views and traditions are the best and become very upset whenever we hear them criticized. If we try to explain our views and others do not accept them, again we become upset. We fail to recognize that each person has his or her own beliefs. It is futile to argue about which view is correct; more beneficial would be to set aside any preconceived notions and to try to see reality. But our attachment to views prevents us from doing so, keeping us unhappy.

Finally, there is attachment to religious forms and ceremonies. We tend to emphasize the external expressions of religion more than their underlying meaning and to feel that anyone who does not perform such ceremonies cannot be a truly religious person. We forget that without its essence, the formal aspect of religion is an empty shell. Piety in reciting prayers or performing ceremonies is valueless if the mind remains filled with anger, passion, and ill will. To be truly religious we must develop the religious attitude: purity of heart, love and compassion for all. But our attachment to the external forms of religion leads us to give more importance to the letter of it than the spirit. We miss the essence of religion and therefore remain miserable.

All our sufferings, whatever they may be, are connected to one or another of these attachments. Attachment and suffering are always found together.

Conditioned Arising: The Chain of Cause and Effect by Which Suffering Originates

What causes attachment? How does it arise? Analyzing his own nature, the future Buddha found that it develops because of the momentary *mental reactions* of liking and disliking. The brief, unconscious reactions of the mind are repeated and intensified moment after moment, growing into powerful attractions and repulsions, into all our attachments. Attachment is merely the developed form of the fleeting reaction. This is the immediate cause of suffering.

What causes reactions of liking and disliking? Looking deeper he saw that they occur because of *sensation*. We feel a pleasant sensation and start liking it; we feel an unpleasant sensation and start disliking it.

Now why these sensations? What causes them? Examining still further within himself he saw that they arise because of *contact:* contact of the eye with a vision, contact of the ear with a sound, contact of the nose with an odor, contact of the tongue with a taste, contact of the body with something tangible, contact of the mind with any thought, emotion, idea, imagination, or memory. Through the five physical senses and the mind we experience the world. Whenever an object or phenomenon contacts any of these six bases of experience, a sensation is produced, pleasant or unpleasant.

And why does contact occur in the first place? The future Buddha saw that because of the existence of the *six sensory bases*—the five physical senses and the mind—contact is bound to occur. The world is full of countless phenomena: sights, sounds, odors, flavors, textures, various thoughts and emotions. So long as our receivers are functioning, contact is inevitable.

Then why do the six sensory bases exist? Because they are essential aspects of the flow of *mind and matter*. And why this flow of mind and matter? What causes it to occur? The future Buddha understood that the process arises because of *consciousness,* the act of cognition which separates the world into the knower and the known, subject and object, "I" and "other." From this separation results identity, "birth." Every moment consciousness arises and assumes a specific mental and physical form. In the next moment, again, consciousness takes a slightly different form. Throughout one's existence, consciousness flows and changes. At last comes death, but consciousness does not stop there: without any interval, in the next moment, it assumes a new form. From one existence to the next, life after life, the flow of consciousness continues.

Then what causes this flow of consciousness? He saw that it arises because of *reaction*. The mind is constantly reacting, and every reaction gives impetus to the flow of consciousness so that it continues to the next moment. The stronger a reaction, the greater the impetus that it gives. The slight reaction of one moment sustains the flow of consciousness only for a moment. But if that momentary reaction of liking and disliking intensifies into craving or aversion, it gains in strength and sustains the flow of consciousness for many moments, for minutes, for hours. And if the reaction of craving and aversion intensifies still further, it sustains the flow for days, for months, perhaps for years. And if throughout life one keeps repeating and intensifying certain reactions, they develop a strength sufficient to sustain the flow of consciousness not only from one moment to the next, from one day to the next, from one year to the next, but from one life to the next.

And what causes these reactions? Observing at the deepest level of reality, he understood that reaction occurs because of *ignorance*. We are unaware of the fact that we react, and unaware of the real nature of what we react to. We are ignorant of the impermanent, impersonal nature of our existence and ignorant that attachment to it brings nothing but suffering. Not knowing our real nature, we react blindly. Not even knowing that we have reacted, we persist in our blind reactions and allow them to intensify. Thus we become imprisoned in the habit of reacting, because of ignorance.

This is how the Wheel of Suffering starts turning:

If ignorance arises, reaction occurs;
if reaction arises, consciousness occurs;
if consciousness arises, mind-and-matter occur;
if mind-and-matter arise, the six senses occur;
if the six senses arise, contact occurs;
if contact arises, sensation occurs;
if sensation arises, craving and aversion occur;
if craving and aversion arise, attachment occurs;
if attachment arises, the process of becoming occurs;
if the process of becoming arises, birth occurs;
if birth arises, decay and death occur, together with sorrow, lamentation, physical and mental suffering, and tribulations.
Thus arises this entire mass of suffering.[3]

By this chain of cause and effect—conditioned arising—we have been brought into our present state of existence and face a future of suffering.

At last the truth was clear to him: suffering begins with ignorance about the reality of our true nature, about the phenomenon labelled "I." And the next cause of suffering is *sankhāra,* the mental habit of reaction. Blinded by ignorance, we generate reactions of craving and aversion, which develop into attachment, leading to all types of unhappiness. The habit of reacting is the *kamma,* the shaper of our future. And the reaction arises only because of ignorance about our real nature. Ignorance, craving, and aversion are the three roots from which grow all our sufferings in life.

The Way out of Suffering

Having understood suffering and its origin, the future Buddha then faced the next question: how can suffering be brought to an end? By remembering the law of *kamma,* of cause and effect: "If this exists, that occurs; that arises from the arising of this. If this does not exist, that does not occur; that ceases from the ceasing of this."[4] Nothing happens without a cause. If the cause is eradicated, there will be no effect. In this way, the process of the arising of suffering can be reversed:

If ignorance is eradicated and completely ceases, reaction ceases;
if reaction ceases, consciousness ceases;
if consciousness ceases, mind-and-matter cease;
if mind-and-matter cease, the six senses cease;
if the six senses cease, contact ceases;
if contact ceases, sensation ceases;
if sensation ceases, craving and aversion cease;
if craving and aversion cease, attachment ceases;
if attachment ceases, the process of becoming ceases;
if the process of becoming ceases, birth ceases;
if birth ceases, decay and death cease, together with sorrow, lamentation, physical and mental suffering and tribulations.
Thus this entire mass of suffering ceases.[5]

If we put an end to ignorance, then there will be no blind reactions that bring in their wake all manner of suffering. And if there is no more suffering, then we shall experience real peace, real happiness. The wheel of suffering can change into the wheel of liberation.

This is what Siddhattha Gotama did in order to achieve enlightenment. This is what he taught others to do. He said,

By yourself committing wrong
you defile yourself.
By yourself not doing wrong
you purify yourself.[6]

We are each responsible for the reactions that cause our suffering. By accepting our responsibility we can learn how to eliminate suffering.

The Flow of Successive Existences

By the Wheel of Conditioned Arising the Buddha explained the process of rebirth or **samsāra**. In the India of his time, this concept was commonly accepted as fact. For many people today, it may seem to be an alien, perhaps untenable, doctrine. Before accepting or rejecting it, however, one should understand what it is and what it is not.

Samsāra is the cycle of repeated existences, the succession of past and future lives. Our deeds are the force that impels us into life after life. Each life, low or high, will be as our deeds were, base or noble. In this respect the concept is not essentially different from that of many religions that teach a future existence where we shall receive retribution or reward for our actions in this life. The Buddha realized, however, that in even the most exalted existence suffering can be found. Therefore we should strive not for a fortunate rebirth, since no rebirth is wholly fortunate. Our aim should rather be liberation from all suffering. When we free ourselves from the cycle of suffering, we experience an unalloyed happiness greater than any worldly pleasure. The Buddha taught a way to experience such happiness in this very life.

Samsāra is not the popular idea of the transmigration of a soul or self that maintains a fixed identity through repeated incarnations. This, the Buddha said, is precisely what does not happen. He insisted that there is no unchanging identity that passes from life to life: "It is just as from the cow comes milk; from milk, curds; from curds, butter; from fresh butter, clarified butter; from clarified butter, the creamy skimmings. When there is milk, it is not considered to be curds, or fresh butter, or clarified butter, or skimmings. Similarly at any time only the present state of existence is considered to be real, and not a past or future one."[7]

The Buddha held neither that a fixed ego-principle is reincarnated in successive lives, nor that there is no past or future existence. Instead he realized and taught that only the process of becoming continues from one existence to another, so long as our actions give impetus to the process.

Even if one believes in no existence other than the present, still the Wheel of Conditioned Arising has relevance. Every moment that we are ignorant of our own blind reactions, we create suffering which we experience here and now. If we remove the ignorance and cease reacting blindly, we shall experience the resulting peace here and now. Heaven and hell exist here and now; they can be experienced within this life, within this body. The Buddha said, "Even if [one believes] there is no other world, no future reward for good actions or punishment for evil ones, still in this very life one can live happily, by keeping oneself free from hatred, ill will, and anxiety."[8]

Regardless of belief or disbelief in past or future existences, we still face the problems of the present life, problems caused by our own blind reactions. Most important for us is to solve these problems now, to take steps toward ending our suffering by ending the habit of reaction, and to experience now the happiness of liberation.

Questions and Answers

QUESTION: *Can't there be wholesome cravings and aversions—for example, hating injustice, desiring freedom, fearing physical harm?*

S. N. GOENKA: Aversions and cravings can never be wholesome. They will always make you tense and unhappy. If you act with craving or aversion in the mind, you may have a worthwhile goal, but you use an unhealthy means to reach it. Of course you have to act to protect yourself from danger. You can do it overpowered by fear, but by doing so you develop a fear complex which will harm you in the long run. Or with hatred in the mind, you may be successful in fighting injustice, but that hatred will become a harmful mental complex. You must fight injustice, you must protect yourself from danger, but you can do so with a balanced mind, without tension. And in a balanced way, you can work to achieve something good, out of love for others. Balance of mind is always helpful and will give the best results.

What is wrong with wanting material things to make life more comfortable?

If it is a real requirement, there is nothing wrong, provided you do not become attached to it. For example, you are thirsty, and you want water; there is nothing unhealthy in that. You need water so you work, get it, and quench your thirst. But if it becomes an obsession, that does not help at all; it harms you. Whatever necessities you require, work to get them. If you fail to get something, then smile and try again in a different way. If you succeed, then enjoy what you get, but without attachment.

How about planning for the future? Would you call that craving?

Again, the criterion is whether you are attached to your plan. Everyone must provide for the future. If your plan does not succeed and you start crying, then you know that you were attached to it. But if you are unsuccessful and can still smile, thinking, "Well, I did my best. So what if I failed? I'll try again!"—then you are working in a detached way, and you remain happy.

Stopping the Wheel of Conditioned Arising sounds like suicide, self-annihilation. Why should we want that?

To seek annihilation of one's life is certainly harmful, just as is the craving to hold on to life. But instead one learns to allow nature to do its work, without craving for anything, not even liberation.

But you said that once the chain of sankhāras *finally stops, then rebirth stops.*

Yes, but that is a far-off story. Concern yourself now with the present life! Don't worry about the future. Make the present good, and the future automatically will be good. Certainly when all *sankhāras* that are responsible for new birth are eliminated, then the process of life and death stops.

Then isn't that annihilation, extinction?

The annihilation of the illusion of "I"; the extinction of suffering. This is the meaning of the word *nibbāna:* the extinction of burning. One is constantly burning in craving, aversion, ignorance. When the burning stops, misery stops. Then what remains is only positive. But to describe it in words is not possible, because it is something beyond the sensory field. It must be experienced in this life; then you know what it is. Then the fear of annihilation will disappear.

What happens to consciousness then?

Why worry about that? It will not help you to speculate about something that can only be experienced, not described. This will only distract you from your real purpose, which is to work to get there. When you reach that stage you will enjoy it, and all the questions will go away. You won't have any more questions! Work to reach that stage.

How can the world function without attachment? If parents were detached then they would not even care about their children. How is it possible to love or to be involved in life without attachment?

Detachment does not mean indifference; it is correctly called "holy indifference." As a parent you must meet your responsibility to care for your child with all your love, but without clinging. Out of love you do your duty. Suppose you tend a sick person, and despite your care, he does not recover. You don't start crying; that would be useless. With a balanced mind, you try to find another way to help him. This is holy indifference: neither inaction nor reaction, but real, positive action with a balanced mind.

Very difficult!

Yes, but this is what you must learn!

The Pebbles and the Ghee

One day a young man came to the Buddha crying and crying; he could not stop. The Buddha asked him, "What is wrong, young man?"

"Sir, yesterday my old father died."

"Well, what can be done? If he has died, crying will not bring him back."

"Yes, sir, that I understand; crying will not bring back my father. But I have come to you, sir, with a special request: please do something for my dead father!"

"Eh? What can I do for your dead father?"

"Sir, please do something. You are such a powerful person, certainly you can do it. Look, these priestlings, pardoners, and almsgatherers perform all sorts of rites and rituals to help the dead. And as soon as the ritual is performed here, the gateway of the kingdom of heaven is breached and the dead person receives entry there; he gets an entry visa. You, sir, are so powerful! If you perform a ritual for my dead father, he will not just receive an entry visa, he'll be granted a permanent stay, a Green Card! Please sir, do something for him!"

The poor fellow was so overwhelmed by grief that he could not follow any rational argument. The Buddha had to use another way to help him understand. So he said to him, "All right. Go to the market and buy two earthen pots." The young man was very happy, thinking that the Buddha had agreed to perform a ritual for his father. He ran to the market and returned with two pots. "All right," the Buddha said, "fill one pot with *ghee*, with butter." The young man did it. "Fill the other with pebbles." He did that too. "Now close their mouths; seal them properly." He did it. "Now place them in the pond over there." The young man did so, and both of the pots sank to the bottom. "Now," said the Buddha, "bring a big stick; strike and break open the pots." The young man was very happy, thinking that the Buddha was performing a wonderful ritual for his father.

According to ancient Indian custom, when a man dies, his son takes the dead body to the cremation ground, puts it on the funeral pyre, and burns it. When the body is half burned, the son takes a thick stick and cracks open the skull. And according to the old belief, as soon as the skull is opened in this world, the gateway of the kingdom of heaven is opened above. So now the young man thought to himself, "The body of my father was burned to ashes yesterday. As a symbol, the Buddha now wants me to break open these pots!" He was very happy with the ritual.

Taking a stick as the Buddha said, the young man struck hard and broke open both the pots. At once the butter contained in one pot came up and started floating on the surface of the water. The pebbles in the other pot spilled out and remained at the bottom. Then the Buddha said, "Well, young man, this much I have done. Now call all your priestlings and miracle workers and tell them to start chanting and praying: 'Oh pebbles, come up, come up! Oh butter, go down, go down!' Let me see how it happens."

"Oh sir, you have started joking! How is it possible, sir? The pebbles are heavier than water, they are bound to stay at the bottom. They can't come up, sir; this is the law of nature! The butter is lighter than water, it is bound to remain on the surface. It can't go down, sir; this is the law of nature!"

"Young man, you know so much about the law of nature, but you have not understood this natural law: if all his life your father performed deeds that were heavy like pebbles, he is bound to go down; who can bring him up? And if all his actions were light like this butter, he is bound to go up; who can pull him down?"

The earlier we understand the law of nature and start living in accordance with the law, the earlier we come out of our misery.'

Chapter 5

THE TRAINING OF
MORAL CONDUCT

Our task is to eradicate suffering by eradicating its causes: ignorance, craving, and aversion. To achieve this goal the Buddha discovered, followed, and taught a practical way to this attainable end. He called this way the Noble Eightfold Path.*

Once, when asked to explain the path in simple words, the Buddha said,

> "Abstain from all unwholesome deeds,
> perform wholesome ones,
> purify your mind"—
> this is the teaching of enlightened persons.[1]

This is a very clear exposition which appears acceptable to all. Everyone agrees that we should avoid actions that are harmful and perform those that are beneficial. But how does one define what is beneficial or harmful, what is wholesome or unwholesome? When we try to do this we rely on our views, our traditional beliefs, our preferences and prejudices, and consequently we produce narrow, sectarian definitions that are acceptable to some but unacceptable to others. Instead of such narrow interpretations the Buddha offered a universal definition of wholesome and unwholesome, of piety and sin. Any action that harms others, that disturbs their peace and harmony, is a sinful action, an unwholesome action. Any action that helps others, that contributes to their peace and harmony, is a pious action, a wholesome action. Further, the mind is truly

---

*For a definition of the Noble Eightfold Path, see Glossary under **ariya atthangika magga**.

purified not by performing religious ceremonies or intellectual exercises, but by experiencing directly the reality of oneself and working systematically to remove the conditioning that gives rise to suffering.

The Noble Eightfold Path can be divided into three stages of training: **sīla, samādhi,** and **paññā.** *Sīla* is moral practice, abstention from all unwholesome actions of body and speech. *Samādhi* is the practice of concentration, developing the ability to consciously direct and control one's own mental processes. *Paññā* is wisdom, the development of purifying insight into one's own nature.

The Value of Moral Practice

Anyone who wishes to practice Dhamma must begin by practicing *sīla.* This is the first step without which one cannot advance. We must abstain from all actions, all words and deeds, that harm other people. This is easily understood; society requires such behavior in order to avoid disruption. But in fact we abstain from such actions not only because they harm others but also because they harm ourselves. It is impossible to commit an unwholesome action—to insult, kill, steal, or rape—without generating great agitation in the mind, great craving and aversion. This moment of craving or aversion brings unhappiness now, and more in the future. The Buddha said,

> Burning now, burning hereafter,
> the wrong-doer suffers doubly. . . .
> Happy now, happy hereafter,
> the virtuous person doubly rejoices.[2]

We need not wait until after death to experience heaven and hell; we can experience them within this life, within ourselves. When we commit unwholesome actions we experience the hell-fire of craving and aversion. When we perform wholesome actions we experience the heaven of inner peace. Therefore it is not only for the benefit of others but for our own benefit, to avoid harm to ourselves, that we abstain from unwholesome words and deeds.

There is another reason for undertaking the practice of *sīla.* We wish to examine ourselves, to gain insight into the depths of our reality. To do this requires a very calm and quiet mind. It is impossible to see into the depths of a pool of water when it is turbulent. Introspection requires a calm mind, free from agitation. Whenever one commits unwholesome action, the mind is inundated with agitation. When one abstains from all unwholesome actions of body or speech, only then does the mind have the opportunity to become peaceful enough so introspection may proceed.

There is still another reason why *sīla* is essential: One who practices Dhamma is working toward the ultimate goal of liberation from all suffering. While performing this task he cannot be involved in actions that will reinforce the very mental habits he seeks to eradicate. Any action that harms others is necessarily caused and accompanied by craving, aversion, and ignorance. Committing such actions is taking two steps back for every step forward on the path, thwarting any progress toward the goal.

Sīla, then, is necessary not only for the good of society but for the good of each of its members, and not only for the worldly good of a person but also for his progress on the path of Dhamma.

Three parts of the Noble Eightfold Path fall within the training of *sīla:* right speech, right action, and right livelihood.

Right Speech

Speech must be pure and wholesome. Purity is achieved by removing impurity, and so we must understand what constitutes impure speech. Such acts include: telling lies, that is, speaking either more or less than the truth; carrying tales that set friends at odds; backbiting and slander; speaking harsh words that disturb others and have no beneficial effect; and idle gossip, meaningless chatter that wastes one's own time and the time of others. Abstaining from all such impure speech leaves nothing but right speech.

Nor is this only a negative concept. One who practices right speech, the Buddha explained,

speaks the truth and is steadfast in truthfulness, trustworthy, dependable, straightforward with others. He reconciles the quarreling and encourages the united. He delights in harmony, seeks after harmony, rejoices in harmony, and creates harmony by his words. His speech is gentle, pleasing to the ear, kindly, heartwarming, courteous, agreeable, and enjoyable to many. He speaks at the proper time, according to the facts, according to what is helpful, according to Dhamma and the Code of Conduct. His words are worth remembering, timely, well-reasoned, well-chosen, and constructive.[3]

Right Action

Action must also be pure. As with speech, we must understand what constitutes impure action so that we may abstain from it. Such acts include: killing a living creature; stealing; sexual misconduct, for example, rape or adultery; and intoxication, losing one's senses so that one does not know what one says or does. Avoiding these four impure actions leaves nothing but right action, wholesome action.

Again this is not only a negative concept. Describing one who practices right physical action the Buddha said, "Laying aside the rod and sword he is careful to harm none, full of kindness, seeking the good of all living creatures. Free of stealth, he himself lives like a pure being."[4]

The Precepts

For ordinary people involved in worldly life, the way to implement right speech and right action is to practice the Five Precepts, which are

1. to abstain from killing any living creature;
2. to abstain from stealing;
3. to abstain from sexual misconduct;
4. to abstain from false speech;
5. to abstain from intoxicants.

These Five Precepts are the essential minimum needed for moral conduct. They must be followed by anyone who wishes to practice Dhamma.

At times during life, however, the opportunity may come to lay aside worldly affairs temporarily—perhaps for a few days, perhaps just for one day—in order to purify the mind, to work toward liberation. Such a period is a time for serious practice of Dhamma, and therefore one's conduct must be more careful than in ordinary life. It is important then to avoid actions that may distract from or interfere with the work of self-purification. Therefore at such a time one follows eight precepts. These include the basic five precepts with one modification: instead of abstaining from sexual misconduct, one abstains from all sexual activities. In addition one undertakes to abstain from untimely eating (that is, from eating after noon); to abstain from all sensual entertainment and bodily decoration; and to abstain from using luxurious beds. The requirement of celibacy and the additional precepts foster the calmness and alertness that are necessary for the work of introspection, and help to free the mind from all external disturbance. The Eight Precepts need be followed only during the time given to intensive practice of Dhamma. When that time is over, a lay person may revert to the Five Precepts as guidelines for moral conduct.

Finally, there are the Ten Precepts for those who have adopted the homeless life of a recluse, a mendicant monk, or a nun. These ten precepts include the first eight, with the seventh precept divided into two and one further precept: to abstain from accepting money. Recluses must support themselves solely by the charity they receive, so that they are free to devote themselves fully to the work of purifying their minds for their own benefit and for the benefit of all.

The precepts, whether five, eight, or ten, are not empty formulas dictated by tradition. They are literally "steps to implement the training," very practical means to ensure that one's speech and actions harm neither others nor oneself.

Right Livelihood

Each person must have a proper way of supporting himself or herself. There are two criteria for right livelihood. First, it should not be necessary to break the Five Precepts in one's work, since doing so obviously causes harm to others. But further, one should not do anything that encourages other people to break the precepts, since this will also cause harm. Neither directly nor indirectly should our means of livelihood involve injury to other beings. Thus any livelihood that requires killing, whether of human beings or of animals, is clearly not right livelihood. But even if the killing is done by others and one simply deals in the parts of slaughtered animals, their skins, flesh, bones, and so on, still this is not right livelihood, because one is depending on the wrong actions of others. Selling liquor or other drugs may be very profitable, but even if one abstains from them oneself, the act of selling encourages others to use intoxicants and thereby to harm themselves. Operating a gambling casino may be very lucrative, but all who come there to gamble cause themselves harm. Selling poisons or weapons—arms, ammunition, bombs, missiles—is good business, but it injures the peace and harmony of multitudes. None of these are right livelihood.

Even though a type of work may not actually harm others, if it is performed with the intention that others should be harmed, it is not right livelihood. The doctor who hopes for an epidemic and the trader who hopes for a famine are not practicing right livelihood.

Each human being is a member of society. We meet our obligations to society by the work we do, serving our fellows in different ways. In return for this we receive our livelihood. Even a monk, a recluse, has his proper work by which he earns the alms he receives: the work of purifying his mind for his good and the benefit of all. If he starts exploiting others by deceiving people, performing feats of magic or falsely claiming spiritual attainments, then he is not practicing right livelihood.

Whatever remuneration we are given in return for our work is to be used for the support of ourselves and our dependents. If there is any excess, at least a portion of it should be returned to society, given to be used for the good of others. If the intention is to play a useful role in society in order to support oneself and to help others, then the work one does is right livelihood.

Practice of *Sīla* in a Course of Vipassana Meditation

Right speech, right action, and right livelihood should be practiced because they make sense for oneself and for others. A course in Vipassana meditation offers the opportunity to apply all these aspects of *sīla*. This is a period set aside for the intensive practice of Dhamma, and therefore the Eight Precepts are followed by all participants. However, one relaxation is allowed for those joining a course for the first time, or for those with medical problems: They are permitted to have a light meal in the evening. For this reason such people formally undertake only the Five Precepts, although in all other respects they actually observe the Eight Precepts.

In addition to the precepts, all participants must take a vow of silence until the last full day of the course. They may speak with the teacher or the course management, but not with other meditators. In this way all distractions are kept to a minimum; people are able to live and work in close quarters without disturbing each other. In this calm, quiet, and peaceful atmosphere it is possible to perform the delicate task of introspection.

In return for performing their work of introspection, meditators receive food and shelter, the cost of which has been donated by others. In this way, during a course they live more or less like true recluses, subsisting on the charity of others. By performing their work to the best of their ability, for their own good and the good of others, the meditators practice right livelihood while participating in a Vipassana course.

The practice of *sīla* is an integral part of the path of Dhamma. Without it there can be no progress on the path, because the mind will remain too agitated to investigate the reality within. There are those who teach that spiritual development is possible without *sīla*. Whatever they may be doing, such people are not following the teaching of the Buddha. Without practicing *sīla* it may be possible to experience various ecstatic states, but it is a mistake to regard these as spiritual attainments. Certainly without *sīla* one can never liberate the mind from suffering and experience ultimate truth.

Questions and Answers

QUESTION: *Isn't performing right action a kind of attachment?*

S. N. GOENKA: No. It is simply doing your best, understanding that the results are beyond your control. You do your job and leave the results to nature, to Dhamma: "Thy will be done."

Then it is being willing to make a mistake?

If you make a mistake you accept it, and try not to repeat it the next time. Again you may fail; again you smile and try a different way. If you can smile in the face of failure, you are not attached. But if failure depresses you and success makes you elated, you are certainly attached.

Then right action is only the effort you make, not the result?

Not the result. That will automatically be good if your action is good. Dhamma takes care of that. We do not have the power to choose the result, but we can choose our actions. Just do the best you can.

Is it wrong action to harm another accidentally?

No. There must be an intention to harm a particular being, and one must succeed in causing harm; only then is wrong action completed. *Sīla* should not be taken to an extreme, which would be neither practical nor beneficial. On the other hand, it is equally dangerous to be so careless in your actions that you keep harming others, and then excuse yourself on the grounds that you had no intention of causing harm. Dhamma teaches us to be mindful.

What is the difference between right and wrong sexual conduct? Is it a question of volition?

No. Sex has a proper place in the life of a householder. It should not be forcibly suppressed, because a forced celibacy produces tensions which create more problems, more difficulties. However, if you give free license to the sexual urge, and allow yourself to have sexual relations with anyone whenever passion arises, then you can never free your mind of passion. Avoiding these two equally dangerous extremes, Dhamma offers a middle path, a healthy expression of sexuality which still permits spiritual development, and that is sexual relations between two people who are committed to each other. And if your partner is also a Vipassana meditator, whenever passion arises you both observe it. This is neither suppression nor free license. By observing you can easily free yourself of passion. At times a couple will still have sexual relations, but gradually they develop toward the stage in which sex has no meaning at all. This is the stage of real, natural celibacy, when not even a thought of passion arises in the mind. This celibacy gives a joy far beyond any sexual satisfaction. Always one feels so contented, so harmonious. One must learn to experience this real happiness.

In the West, many think that sexual relations between any two consenting adults are permissible.

That view is far away from Dhamma. Someone who has sex with one person, than another, and then someone else, is multiplying his passion, his misery. You must be either committed to one person or living in celibacy.

How about the use of drugs as aids to experience other types of consciousness, different realities?

Some students have told me that by using psychedelic drugs they passed through experiences similar to those they encountered in meditation. Whether or not this is really so, having a drug-induced experience is a form of dependence on an outside agency. Dhamma, however, teaches you to become your own master so that you can experience reality at will, whenever you wish. And another very important difference is that the use of drugs causes many people to lose their mental balance and to harm themselves, while the experience of truth by the practice of Dhamma causes meditators to become more balanced, without harming themselves or anyone else.

Is the fifth precept to abstain from intoxicants or to abstain from becoming intoxicated? After all, drinking in moderation, without becoming drunk, does not seem particularly harmful. Or are you saying that drinking even one glass of alcohol is breaking sīla?

By drinking even a small amount, in the long run you develop a craving for alcohol. You don't realize it but you take a first step toward addiction, which is certainly harmful to yourself and others. Every addict starts by taking just one glass. Why take the first step toward suffering? If you practice meditation seriously and one day you drink a glass of wine out of forgetfulness or at a social gathering, that day you will find that your meditation is weak. Dhamma cannot go together with the use of intoxicants. If you really wish to develop in Dhamma, you must stay free from all intoxicants. This is the experience of thousands of meditators.

The two precepts concerning sexual misconduct and the use of intoxicants particularly need to be understood by people from Western countries.

People here often say, "If it feels good, it must be right."

Because they don't see reality. When you perform an action out of aversion, automatically you are aware of agitation in the mind. When, however, you perform an action out of craving, it seems pleasant at the surface level of the mind, but there is an agitation at a deeper level. You feel good only out of ignorance. When you realize how you harm yourself by such actions, naturally you stop committing them.

Is it breaking sīla *to eat meat?*

No, not unless you have killed the animal yourself. If meat happens to be provided for you and you enjoy its taste as you would that of any other food, you have not broken any precept. But of course by eating meat you indirectly encourage someone else to break the precepts by killing. And also at a subtler level you harm yourself by eating meat. Every moment an animal generates craving and aversion; it is incapable of observing itself, of purifying its mind. Every fiber of its body becomes permeated with craving and aversion. This is the input you receive when eating non-vegetarian food. A meditator is trying to eradicate craving and aversion, and therefore would find it helpful to avoid such food.

Is that why only vegetarian food is served at a course?

Yes, because it is best for Vipassana meditation.

Do you recommend vegetarianism in daily life?

That is also helpful.

How can making money be acceptable conduct for a meditator?

If you practice Dhamma, you are happy even if you don't make money. But if you make money and do not practice Dhamma, you remain unhappy. Dhamma is more important. As someone living in the world, you have to support yourself. You must earn money by honest, hard work; there is nothing wrong in that. But do it with Dhamma.

If somewhere down the road your work may have an effect that is not good, if what you do can be used in a negative way, is that wrong livelihood?

It depends on your intention. If you are concerned only to accumulate money, if you think, "Let others be harmed, I don't care so long as I get my money," this is wrong livelihood. But if your intention is to serve and nevertheless someone is harmed, you are not to blame for that.

My company produces an instrument that, among other things, is used to gather data on atomic explosions. They asked me to work on this product, and somehow it did not seem right to me.

If something will be used only for harming others, certainly you should not be involved in that. But if it can be used for positive as well as negative purposes, you are not responsible for the use others make of it. You do your work with the intention that others should use this for a good purpose. There is nothing wrong with that.

What do you think of pacifism?

If by pacifism you mean inaction in the face of aggression, certainly that is wrong. Dhamma teaches you to act in a positive way, to be practical.

How about the use of passive resistance, as taught by Mahatma Gandhi or Martin Luther King, Jr.?

It depends on the situation. If an aggressor can understand no other language except force, one must use physical strength, always maintaining equanimity. Otherwise one should use passive resistance, not out of fear but as an act of moral bravery. This is the Dhamma way, and this is what Gandhiji trained people to do. It requires courage to face with empty hands the aggression of armed opponents. To do that one must be prepared to die. Death is bound to come sooner or later; one can die in fear or bravely. A Dhamma death cannot be in fear. Gandhiji used to tell his followers who faced violent opposition, "Let your wounds be on your chests, not on your backs." He succeeded because of the Dhamma in him.

You yourself say that people can have wonderful meditation experiences without maintaining the precepts. Isn't it then dogmatic and inflexible to put so much stress on moral conduct?

I have seen from the case of a number of students that people who give no importance to *sīla* cannot make any progress on the path. For years such people may come to courses and have wonderful experiences in meditation, but in their daily lives there is no change. They remain agitated and miserable because they are only playing a game with Vipassana, as they have played so many other games. Such people are real losers. Those who really want to use Dhamma in order to change their lives for better must practice *sīla* as carefully as possible.

The Doctor's Prescription

A man becomes sick and goes to the doctor for help. The doctor examines him and then writes out a prescription for some medicine. The man has great faith in his doctor. He returns home and in his prayer room he puts a beautiful picture or statue of the doctor. Then he sits down and pays respects to that picture or statue: he bows down three times, and offers flowers and incense. And then he takes out the prescription that the doctor wrote for him, and very solemnly he recites it: "Two pills in the morning! Two pills in the afternoon! Two pills in the evening!" All day, all life long he keeps reciting the prescription because he has great faith in the doctor, but still the prescription does not help him.

The man decides that he wants to know more about this prescription, and so he runs to the doctor and asks him, "Why did you prescribe this medicine? How will it help me?" Being an intelligent person, the doctor explains, "Well, look, this is your disease, and this is the root cause of your disease. If you take the medicine I have prescribed, it will eradicate the cause of your disease. When the cause is eradicated, the disease will automatically disappear." The man thinks, "Ah, wonderful! My doctor is so intelligent! His prescriptions are so helpful!" And he goes home and starts fighting with his neighbors and acquaintances, insisting, "My doctor is the best doctor! All other doctors are useless!" But what does he gain by such arguments? All his life he may continue fighting, but still this does not help him at all. If he *takes* the medicine, only then will the man be relieved of his misery, his disease. Only then will the medicine help him.

Every liberated person is like a physician. Out of compassion, he gives a prescription advising people how to free themselves of suffering. If people develop blind faith in that person, they turn the prescription into a scripture and start fighting with other sects, claiming that the teaching of the founder of their religion is superior. But no one cares to practice the teaching, to take the medicine prescribed in order to eliminate the malady.

Having faith in the doctor is useful if it encourages the patient to follow his advice. Understanding how the medicine works is beneficial if it encourages one to take the medicine. But without actually taking the medicine, one cannot be cured of the disease. You have to take the medicine yourself.

Chapter 6

THE TRAINING OF
CONCENTRATION

By practicing *sīla* we attempt to control our speech and physical actions. However, the cause of suffering lies in our mental actions. Merely restraining our words and deeds is useless if the mind continues to boil in craving and aversion, in unwholesome mental actions. Divided against ourselves in this way, we can never be happy. Sooner or later the craving and aversion will erupt and we shall break *sīla*, harming others and ourselves.

Intellectually one may understand that it is wrong to commit unwholesome actions. After all, for thousands of years every religion has preached the importance of morality. But when the temptation comes, it overpowers the mind and one breaks *sīla*. An alcoholic may know perfectly well that he should not drink because alcohol is harmful to him, and yet when the craving arises he reaches for the alcohol and becomes intoxicated. He cannot stop himself, because he has no control over his mind. But when one learns to cease committing unwholesome *mental* actions, it becomes easy to refrain from unwholesome words and deeds.

Because the problem originates in the mind, we must confront it at the mental level. In order to do so, we must undertake the practice of **bhāvanā**—literally, "mental development," or, in common language, meditation. Since the time of the Buddha, the meaning of the word *bhāvanā* has become vague as the practice of it has fallen away. In recent times, it has been used to refer to any sort of mental culture or spiritual uplift, even such activities as reading, talking, hearing, or thinking about Dhamma. "Meditation," the most common English translation of *bhāvanā*, is used even more loosely to refer to many activities, from mental relaxation, day-dreaming, and free association, to self-hypnosis. All these are far from what the Buddha meant by *bhāvanā*. He used the term to refer to specific mental exercises, precise techniques for focusing and purifying the mind.

Bhāvanā includes the two trainings of concentration (*samādhi*) and wisdom (*paññā*). The practice of concentration is also called "the development of tranquility" (**samatha-bhāvanā**), and that of wisdom is called "the development of insight" (**vipassanā-bhāvanā**). The practice of *bhāvanā* begins with concentration, which is the second division of the Noble Eightfold Path. This is the wholesome action of learning to take control of the mental processes, to become master of one's own mind. Three parts of the path fall within this training: right effort, right awareness, and right concentration.

Right Effort

Right effort is the first step in the practice of *bhāvanā*. The mind is easily overcome by ignorance, easily swayed by craving or aversion. Somehow we must strengthen it so that it becomes firm and stable, a useful tool for examining our nature at the subtlest level in order to reveal and then remove our conditioning.

A doctor, wishing to diagnose the disease of a patient, will take a blood sample and place it under a microscope. Before examining the sample, the doctor must first focus the microscope properly, and fix it in focus. Only then is it possible to inspect the sample, discover the cause of the disease and determine the proper treatment to cure the disease. Similarly, we must learn to focus the mind, to fix and maintain it on a single object of attention. In this way we make it an instrument for examining the subtlest reality of ourselves.

The Buddha prescribed various techniques for concentrating the mind, each suited to the particular person who came to him for training. The most suitable technique for exploring inner reality, the technique the Buddha himself practiced, is that of **ānāpana-sati**, "awareness of respiration."

Respiration is an object of attention that is readily available to everyone, because we all breathe from the time of birth until the time of death. It is a universally accessible, universally acceptable object of meditation. To begin the practice of *bhāvanā,* meditators sit down, assume a comfortable, upright posture, and close their eyes. They should be in a quiet room with little to distract the attention. Turning from the outer world to the world within, they find that the most prominent activity is their own breathing; so they give attention to this object: the breath entering and leaving the nostrils.

This is not a breathing exercise; it is an exercise in awareness. The effort is not to control the breath but instead to remain conscious of it as it naturally is: long or short, heavy or light, rough or subtle. For as long as possible one fixes the attention on the breath, without allowing any distractions to break the chain of awareness.

As meditators we find out at once how difficult this is. As soon as we try to keep the mind fixed on respiration, we begin to worry about a pain in the legs. As soon as we try to suppress all distracting thoughts, a thousand things jump into the mind: memories, plans, hopes, fears. One of these catches our attention, and after some time we realize that we have forgotten completely about breathing. We begin again with renewed determination, and again after a short time we realize that the mind has slipped away without our noticing.

Who is in control here? As soon as one begins this exercise, it becomes very clear very quickly that in fact the mind is out of control. Like a spoiled child who reaches for one toy, becomes bored, and reaches for another, and then another, the mind keeps jumping from one thought, one object of attention to another, running away from reality.

This is the ingrained habit of the mind; this is what it has been doing all our lives. But once we start to investigate our true nature, the running away must stop. We must change the mental habit pattern and learn to remain with reality. We begin by trying to fix the attention on the breath. When we notice that it has wandered away, patiently and calmly we bring it back again. We fail and try again, and again. Smilingly, without tension, without discouragement, we keep repeating the exercise. After all, the habit of a lifetime is not changed in a few minutes. The task requires repeated, continuous practice as well as patience and calmness. This is how we develop awareness of reality. This is right effort.

The Buddha described four types of right effort:

• to prevent evil, unwholesome states from arising;
• to abandon them if they should arise;
• to generate wholesome states not yet existing;
• to maintain them without lapse, causing them to develop and to reach full growth and perfection.[1]

By practicing awareness of respiration, we practice all four right efforts. We sit down and fix attention on the breath without any intervening thought. By doing so, we initiate and maintain the wholesome state of self-awareness. We prevent ourselves from falling into distraction, or absent-mindedness, from losing sight of reality. If a thought arises, we do not pursue it, but return our attention once again to the breath. In this way, we develop the ability of the mind to remain focused on a single object and to resist distractions—two essential qualities of concentration.

Right Awareness

Observing respiration is also the means for practicing right awareness. Our suffering stems from ignorance. We react because we do not know what we are doing, because we do not know the reality of ourselves. The mind spends most of the time lost in fantasies and illusions, reliving pleasant or unpleasant experiences and anticipating the future with eagerness or fear. While lost in such cravings or aversions we are unaware of what is happening now, what we are doing now. Yet surely this moment, now, is the most important for us. We cannot live in the past; it is gone. Nor can we live in the future; it is forever beyond our grasp. We can live only in the present.

If we are unaware of our present actions, we are condemned to repeating the mistakes of the past and can never succeed in attaining our dreams for the future. But if we can develop the ability to be aware of the present moment, we can use the past as a guide for ordering our actions in the future, so that we may attain our goal.

Dhamma is the path of here-and-now. Therefore we must develop our ability to be aware of the present moment. We require a method to focus our attention on our own reality in this moment. The technique of *ānāpāna-sati* is such a method. Practicing it develops awareness of oneself in the here-and-now: at this moment breathing in, at this moment breathing out. By practicing awareness of respiration, we become aware of the present moment.

Another reason for developing awareness of respiration is that we wish to experience ultimate reality. Focusing on breathing can help us explore whatever is unknown about ourselves, to bring into consciousness whatever has been unconscious. It acts as a bridge between the conscious and unconscious mind, because the breath functions both consciously and unconsciously. We can decide to breathe in a particular way, to control the respiration. We can even stop breathing for a time. And yet when we cease trying to control respiration, it continues without any prompting.

For example, we may begin by breathing intentionally, slightly hard, in order to fix the attention more easily. As soon as the awareness of respiration becomes clear and steady, we allow the breath to proceed naturally, either hard or soft, deep or shallow, long or short, fast or slow. We make no effort to regulate the breath; the effort is only to be aware of it. By maintaining awareness of natural breath we have started observing the autonomic functioning of the body, an activity which is usually unconscious. From observing the gross reality of intentional breathing, we have progressed to observing the subtler reality of natural breathing. We have begun to move beyond superficial reality toward awareness of a subtler reality.

Yet another reason for developing awareness of respiration is in order to become free of craving, aversion, and ignorance, by first becoming aware of them. In this task the breath can help, because respiration acts as a reflection of one's mental state. When the mind is peaceful and calm, the breath is regular and gentle. But whenever negativity arises in the mind, whether anger, hatred, fear, or passion, then respiration becomes more rough, heavy, and rapid. In this way, our respiration alerts us to our mental state and enables us to start to deal with it.

There is yet another reason for practicing awareness of breathing. Since our goal is a mind free of negativity, we must be careful that every step we take toward that goal is pure and wholesome. Even in the initial stage of developing *samādhi* we must use an object of attention which is wholesome. Breath is such an object. We cannot have craving or aversion toward the breath, and it is a reality, totally divorced from illusion or delusion. Therefore it is an appropriate object of attention.

In the moment when the mind is fully focused on respiration, it is free from craving, free of aversion, and free of ignorance. However brief that moment of purity may be, it is very powerful, for it challenges all one's past conditioning. All the accumulated reactions are stirred up and begin to appear as various difficulties, physical as well as mental, which hinder one's efforts to develop awareness. We may experience impatience for progress, which is a form of craving; or else aversion may arise in the form of anger and depression because progress seems slow. Sometimes lethargy overwhelms us and we doze off as soon as we sit to meditate. Sometimes we may be so agitated that we fidget or find excuses to avoid meditating. Sometimes skepticism undermines the will to work—obsessive, unreasoning doubts about the teacher, or the teaching, or our own ability to meditate. When suddenly faced with these difficulties, we may think of giving up the practice altogether.

At such a moment we must understand that these hindrances have arisen only in reaction to our success in practicing awareness of respiration. If we persevere they will gradually disappear. When they do, the work becomes easier, because even at this early stage of practice, some layers of conditioning have been eradicated from the surface of the mind. In this way, even as we practice awareness of breathing, we begin to cleanse the mind and advance toward liberation.

Right Concentration

Fixing the attention on respiration develops awareness of the present moment. Maintaining this awareness from moment to moment, for as long as possible, is right concentration.

In the daily actions of ordinary life, concentration is also required, but it is not necessarily the same as right concentration. A person may be concentrating on satisfying a sensual desire or forestalling a fear. A cat waits with all its attention focused on a mousehole, ready to pounce as soon as a mouse appears. A pickpocket is intent on the victim's wallet, waiting for the moment to remove it. A child in bed at night stares fearfully at the darkest corner of the room, imagining monsters hidden in the shadows.

None of these is right concentration, concentration that can be used for liberation. *Samādhi* must have as its focus an object that is free from all craving, all aversion, all illusion.

In practicing awareness of breathing one finds how difficult it is to maintain unbroken awareness. Despite a firm determination to keep the attention fixed on the object of the breath, somehow it slips away unnoticed. We find we are like a drunken man trying to walk a straight line, who keeps straying to one side or the other. In fact we *are* drunk with our own ignorance and illusions, and so we keep straying into past or future, craving or aversion. We cannot remain on the straight path of sustained awareness.

As meditators, we would be wise not to become depressed or discouraged when faced with these difficulties, but instead to understand that it takes time to change the ingrained mental habits of years. It can be done only by working repeatedly, continuously, patiently, and persistently. Our job is simply to return attention to our breathing as soon as we notice that it has strayed. If we can do that, we have taken an important step toward changing the wandering ways of the mind. And by repeated practice, it becomes possible to bring the attention back more and more quickly. Gradually, the periods of forgetfulness become shorter and the periods of sustained awareness—*samādhi*—become longer.

As concentration strengthens, we begin to feel relaxed, happy, full of energy. Little by little the breath changes, becoming soft, regular, light, shallow. At times it may seem that respiration has stopped altogether. Actually, as the mind becomes tranquil, the body also becomes calm and the metabolism slows down, so that less oxygen is required.

At this stage some of those who practice awareness of respiration may have various unusual experiences: seeing lights or visions while sitting with eyes closed or hearing extraordinary sounds, for example. All these so-called extrasensory experiences are merely indications that the mind has attained a heightened level of concentration. In themselves these phenomena have no importance and should be given no attention. The object of awareness remains respiration; anything else is a distraction. Nor should one expect such experiences; they occur in some cases and not in others. All these extraordinary experiences are simply milestones that mark progress on the path. Sometimes the milestone may be hidden from view, or we may be so intent on the path that we stride ahead without noticing it. But if we take such a milestone as the final goal and cling to it, we cease making progress altogether. After all, there are countless extraordinary sensory experiences to be had. Those practicing Dhamma are not seeking such experiences but rather insight into their own nature, so as to attain freedom from suffering.

Therefore we continue to give attention only to respiration. As the mind becomes more concentrated, the breath becomes finer and more difficult to follow, thereby requiring still greater efforts to remain attentive. In this way we continue to hone the mind, to sharpen the concentration, to make of it a tool with which to penetrate beyond apparent reality in order to observe the subtlest reality within.

There are many other techniques to develop concentration. One may be taught to concentrate on a word by repeating it, or on a visual image, or even to perform over and over again a certain physical action. In doing so one becomes absorbed in the object of attention, and attains a blissful state of trance. Although such a state is no doubt very pleasant so long as it lasts, when it ends one finds oneself back in ordinary life with the same problems as before. These techniques work by developing a layer of peace and joy at the surface of the mind, but in the depths the conditioning remains untouched. The objects used to attain concentration in such techniques have no connection with the moment-to-moment reality of oneself. The bliss that one attains is superimposed, intentionally created, rather than arising spontaneously from the depths of a purified mind. Right *samādhi* cannot be spiritual intoxication. It must be free from all artificiality, all illusions.

Even within the teaching of the Buddha, there are various states of trance—**jhāna**—that can be attained. The Buddha himself was taught eight states of mental absorption before he became enlightened, and he continued to practice them throughout his life. However, states of trance alone could not liberate him. When he taught the states of absorption, therefore, he emphasized their function only as stepping-stones to the development of insight. Meditators develop the faculty of concentration not in order to experience bliss or ecstasy, but rather to forge the mind into an instrument with which to examine their own reality and to remove the conditioning that causes their suffering. This is right concentration.

Questions and Answers

QUESTION: *Why do you teach students to practice* ānāpāna *concentrating on the nostrils rather than on the belly?*

S. N. GOENKA: Because for us *ānāpāna* is practiced as a preparation for the practice of Vipassana, and in this type of Vipassana a particularly strong concentration is necessary. The more limited the area of attention, the stronger the concentration will be. For developing concentration to this degree, the abdomen is too large. Most suitable is the area of the nostrils. That is why the Buddha guided us to work in this area.

While practicing awareness of respiration, is it permissible to count breaths, or to say "in" as we breathe in and "out" as we breathe out?

No, there should be no continuous verbalization. If all the time you add a word to the awareness of respiration, gradually the word will become predominant and you will forget about the breath entirely. Then whether you breathe in or out, you will say "In!" Whether you breathe out or in, you will say "Out!" The word will become a mantra. Just remain with the breath, bare breath, nothing but breath.

Why is the practice of samādhi *not sufficient for liberation?*

Because the purity of mind developed through *samādhi* is achieved primarily by suppression, not elimination of conditioning. It is just as if someone cleans a tank of muddy water by adding a precipitating agent, for example, alum. The alum causes the mud particles suspended in the water to fall to the bottom of the tank, leaving the water crystal-clear. Similarly *samādhi* makes the upper levels of the mind crystal-clear, but a deposit of impurities remains in the unconscious. These latent impurities must be removed in order to reach liberation. And to remove the impurities from the depths of the mind, one must practice Vipassana.

Isn't it harmful to forget the past and future entirely and to give attention only to the present moment? After all, isn't that the way animals live? Surely whoever forgets the past is condemned to repeat it.

This technique will not teach you to forget the past entirely or to have no concern for the future. But the present mental habit pattern is to immerse oneself constantly in past memories or in cravings, plans, or fears for the future, and to remain ignorant of the present. This unhealthy habit makes life miserable. By meditation you learn to keep a firm foothold in the present reality. With this solid base you can take the necessary guidance from the past and make proper provision for the future.

I find that when I meditate and the mind wanders, a craving may start, and then I think I'm not supposed to crave, and I start getting agitated because I am craving. How should I deal with this?

Why get agitated because of the craving? Just accept the fact: "Look, there is craving"—that's all. And you will come out of it. When you find that the mind has wandered, you accept: "Look, the mind has wandered," and automatically it will return to respiration. Don't create tensions because there is craving or because the mind has wandered; if you do that, you generate fresh aversion. Just accept it. This acceptance is enough.

All Buddhist meditation techniques were already known in yoga. What was truly new in meditation as taught by the Buddha?

What is called yoga today is actually a later development. Patanjali lived about 500 years after the time of the Buddha, and naturally his *Yoga Sūtra* shows the influence of the Buddha's teachings. Of course yogic practices were known in India even before the Buddha, and he himself experimented with them before achieving enlightenment. All these practices, however, were limited to *sīla* and *samādhi*, concentration up to the level of the eighth *jhāna*, the eighth stage of absorption, which is still within the field of sensory experience. The Buddha found the ninth *jhāna*, and that is Vipassana, the development of insight that will take the meditator to the ultimate goal beyond all sensory experience.

I find that I am very quick to belittle other people. What is the best way to work with this problem?

Work with it by meditating. If the ego is strong, one will try to belittle others, to lower their importance and increase one's own. But meditation naturally dissolves the ego. When it dissolves, you can no longer do anything to hurt another. Work and the problem will automatically be solved.

At times I feel guilty about what I have done.

Feeling guilty will not help you; it will only cause harm. Guilt has no place on the path of Dhamma. When you realize that you have acted in a wrong way, simply accept the fact without trying to justify or conceal it. You may go to someone you respect and say, "Well, I made this mistake. In future I'll be careful not to repeat it." And then meditate, and you will find that you can come out of the difficulty.

Why do I keep reinforcing this ego? Why do I keep trying to be "I"?

This is what the mind has been conditioned to do, out of ignorance. But Vipassana can liberate you from this harmful conditioning. In place of always thinking of self, you learn to think of others.

How does that happen?

The first step is to recognize how selfish and egocentric one is. Unless someone realizes this truth, he cannot emerge from the madness of self-love. As you practice more, you will realize that even your love for others is in fact self-love. You will understand, "Whom do I love? I love someone because I expect something from that person. I expect him to behave in a way that I like. The moment he starts to behave in a different way, all my love is gone. Then do I really love this person or myself?" The answer will become clear, not by intellectualizing, but by your practice of Vipassana. And once you have this direct realization, you begin to emerge from your selfishness. Then you learn to develop real love for others, love that is selfless, one-way traffic: giving without expecting anything in return.

I work in an area where there are a lot of street people who hold out their hands and say, "Spare change?"

So it is also in the West? I thought begging is found only in poor countries!

I know that many of these street people are on drugs. I wonder if by giving them money, we encourage them to use drugs.

That is why you must take care that any donation you give will be properly used. Otherwise it doesn't help anybody. Instead of giving such people money, if you help them come out of their addictions, then you do them real service. Whatever action you perform must be with wisdom.

When you say "Be happy," the other side of that to me is "Be sad."

Why be sad? Come out of sadness!

Right, but I thought we were working for balance.

The balance makes you happy. If you are unbalanced, you are sad. Be balanced; be happy!

I thought it was "Be balanced, be no thing."

No, no. Balance makes you happy, not nothing. You become positive when you have a balanced mind.

The Crooked Milk Pudding

Two young boys, who were very poor, lived by begging for their food from house to house in the city and in the countryside. One of them was blind from birth, and the other helped him; in this way they made their rounds together, begging for food.

One day the blind boy fell sick. His companion said, "Stay here and rest. I'll go round to beg for us both, and I'll bring the food back for you." And he went off to beg.

That day it so happened that the boy was given a very delicious dish: *khir,* Indian-style milk pudding. He had never tasted this dish before and enjoyed it very much. But unfortunately he had no container in which to bring the pudding back to his friend, so he ate it all.

When he came back to his blind companion, the boy said, "I am so sorry, today I was given a wonderful dish, milk pudding, but I could not bring any back for you."

The blind boy asked him, "What is this milk pudding?"

"Oh, it is white. Milk is white."

Being blind from birth, his companion did not understand. "What is white?"

"Don't you know what white is?"

"No, I don't."

"It's the opposite of black."

"Then what is black?" He did not know what black was either.

"Oh, try to understand, white!" But the blind boy could not understand. So his friend looked about him and seeing a white crane, he caught hold of the bird and brought it to the blind boy saying, "White is like this bird."

Not having eyes, the blind boy reached out to touch the crane with his fingers. "Ah, now I understand what white is! It is soft."

"No, no, it has nothing to do with being soft. White is white! Try to understand."

"But you told me it is like this crane, and I examined the crane and it is soft. So the milk pudding is soft. White means soft."

"No, you have not understood. Try again."

Again the blind boy examined the crane, passing his hand from the beak to the neck, to the body, to the tip of the tail. "Oh, now I understand. It is crooked! The milk pudding is crooked!"

He cannot understand because he does not have the faculty to experience what white is. In the same way, if you do not have the faculty to experience reality as it is, it will always be crooked for you.

Chapter 7

THE TRAINING OF WISDOM

Neither *sīla* nor *samādhi* is unique to the teaching of the Buddha. Both were well known and practiced before his enlightenment; in fact, while searching for the way to liberation, the future Buddha was trained in *samādhi* by two teachers with whom he studied. In prescribing these trainings the Buddha did not differ from the teachers of conventional religion. All religions insist on the necessity of moral behavior, and they also offer the possibility of attaining states of bliss, whether by prayer, by rituals, by fasting and other austerities, or by various forms of meditation. The goal of such practices is simply a state of deep mental absorption. This is the "ecstasy" experienced by religious mystics.

Such concentration, even if not developed to the level of the trance states, is very helpful. It calms the mind by diverting attention from the situations in which one would otherwise react with craving and aversion. Counting slowly to ten to prevent an outburst of anger is a rudimentary form of *samādhi*. Other, perhaps more obvious, forms are repetition of a word or mantra, or concentration on a visual object. They all work: When the attention is diverted to a different object, the mind appears to become calm and peaceful.

The calm achieved in this way, however, is not real liberation. Certainly the practice of concentration confers great benefits, but it works only at the conscious level of the mind. Nearly twenty-five centuries before the invention of modern psychology, the Buddha realized the existence of the unconscious mind, which he called the **anusaya**. Diverting the attention, he found, is a way to deal effectively with craving and aversion at the conscious level, but it does not actually eliminate them. Instead it pushes them deep into the unconscious, where they remain as dangerous as ever even though dormant. At the surface level of the mind there may be a layer of peace and harmony, but in the depths is a sleeping volcano of suppressed negativity which sooner or later will erupt violently. The Buddha said,

> If the roots remain untouched and firm in the ground,
> a felled tree still puts forth new shoots.
> If the underlying habit of craving and aversion is not uprooted,
> suffering arises anew over and over again.[1]

So long as conditioning remains in the unconscious mind, it will put forth fresh shoots at the first opportunity, causing suffering. For this reason, even after reaching the highest states attainable by the practice of concentration, the future Buddha was not satisfied that he had achieved liberation. He decided that he must continue his search for the way out of suffering and the path to happiness.

He saw two choices. The first is the path of self-indulgence, of giving oneself free license to seek the satisfaction of all one's desires. This is the worldly path which most people follow, whether they realize it or not. But he saw clearly that it cannot lead to happiness. There is no one in the universe whose desires are always fulfilled, in whose life everything that is wished for happens and nothing happens that is not wished. People who follow this path inevitably suffer when they fail to achieve their desires; that is, they suffer disappointment and dissatisfaction. But they suffer equally when they attain their desires: they suffer from the fear that the desired object will vanish, that the moment of gratification will prove transitory, as in fact it must. In seeking, in attaining, and in missing their desires, such people always remain agitated. The future Buddha had experienced this path himself before leaving worldly life to become a recluse, and therefore he knew that it cannot be the way to peace.

The alternative is the path of self-restraint, of deliberately refraining from satisfying one's desires. In India 2500 years ago, this path of self-denial was taken to the extreme of avoiding all pleasurable experiences and inflicting on oneself unpleasurable ones.

The rationale for this self-punishment was that it would cure the habit of craving and aversion and thereby purify the mind. The practice of such austerities is a phenomenon of religious life throughout the world. The future Buddha had experienced this path as well in the years following his adoption of the homeless life. He had tried different ascetic practices to the point that his body was reduced to skin and bones, but still he found that he was not liberated. Punishing the body does not purify the mind.

Self-restraint need not be carried to such an extreme, however. One may practice it in more moderate form by abstaining from gratifying those desires that would involve unwholesome actions. This kind of self-control seems far preferable to self-indulgence since in practicing it, one would at least avoid immoral actions. But if self-restraint is achieved only by self-repression, it will increase the mental tensions to a dangerous degree. All the suppressed desires will accumulate like floodwater behind the dam of self-denial. One day the dam is bound to break and release a destructive flood.

So long as conditioning remains in the mind, we cannot be secure or at peace. *Sīla,* beneficial though it is, cannot be maintained by sheer force of will. Developing *samādhi* will help, but this is only a partial solution that will not work at the depths of the mind where the roots of the problem lie, the roots of the impurities. So long as these roots remain buried in the unconscious, there can be no real, lasting happiness, no liberation.

But if the roots of conditioning themselves can be removed from the mind, then there will be no danger of indulgence in unwholesome actions, no necessity for self-repression, because the very impulse for performing unwholesome action will be gone. Freed of the tensions either of seeking or denying, one can live at peace.

To remove the roots a method is required with which we can penetrate to the depths of the mind in order to deal with the impurities where they begin. This method is what the Buddha found: the training of wisdom, or *paññā,* which led him to enlightenment. It is also called *vipassanā-bhāvanā,* the development of insight into one's own nature, insight by means of which one may recognize and eliminate the causes of suffering. This was the discovery of the Buddha—what he practiced for his own liberation, and what he taught others throughout his life. This is the unique element in his teachings, to which he gave the highest importance. He repeatedly said, "If it is supported by morality, concentration is very fruitful, very beneficial. If it is supported by concentration, wisdom is very fruitful, very beneficial. If it is supported by wisdom, the mind becomes freed of all defilements."[2]

In themselves, morality and concentration, *sīla* and *samādhi,* are valuable, but their real purpose is to lead to wisdom. It is only in developing *paññā* that we find a true middle path between the extremes of self-indulgence and self-repression. By practicing morality, we avoid actions that cause the grossest forms of mental agitation. By concentrating the mind, we further calm it and at the same time shape it into an effective tool with which to undertake the work of self-examination. But it is only by developing wisdom that we can penetrate into the reality within and free ourselves of all ignorance and attachments.

Two parts of the Noble Eightfold Path are included within the training of wisdom: right thought and right understanding.

Right Thought

It is not necessary for all thoughts to cease in meditation before one begins *vipassanā-bhāvanā.* Thoughts may still persist, but if awareness is sustained from moment to moment, that is sufficient to start the work.

Thoughts may remain, but the nature of the thought pattern changes. Aversion and craving have been calmed down by awareness of breathing. The mind has become tranquil at least at the conscious level, and has begun to think about Dhamma, about the way to emerge from suffering. The difficulties that arose on initiating awareness of respiration have now passed or at least have been overcome to some extent. One is prepared for the next step, right understanding.

Right Understanding

It is right understanding that is real wisdom. Thinking about truth is not enough. We must realize truth ourselves, we must see things as they really are, not just as they appear to be. Apparent truth is a reality, but one that we must penetrate in order to experience the ultimate reality of ourselves and eliminate suffering.

There are three kinds of wisdom: received wisdom (**suta-mayā paññā**), intellectual wisdom (**cintā-mayā paññā**), and experiential wisdom (**bhāvanā-mayā paññā**). The literal meaning of the phrase **suta-mayā paññā** is "heard wisdom"—wisdom learned from others, by reading books or listening to sermons or lectures, for example. This is another person's wisdom which one decides to adopt as one's own. The acceptance may be out of ignorance. For example, people who have grown up in a community with a certain ideology, a system of beliefs, religious or otherwise, may accept without questioning the ideology of the community. Or the acceptance may be out of craving. Leaders of the community may declare that accepting the established ideology, the traditional beliefs, will guarantee a wonderful future; perhaps they claim that all believers will attain heaven after death. Naturally the bliss of heaven is very attractive, and so willingly one accepts. Or the acceptance may be out of fear. Leaders may see that people have doubts and questions about the ideology of the community, so they warn them to conform to the commonly held beliefs, threatening them with terrible punishment in the future if they do not conform, perhaps claiming that all unbelievers will go to hell after death. Naturally, people do not want to go to hell, so they swallow their doubts and adopt the beliefs of the community.

Whether it is accepted out of blind faith, out of craving, or out of fear, received wisdom is not one's own wisdom, not something experienced for oneself. It is borrowed wisdom.

The second type of wisdom is intellectual understanding. After reading or hearing a certain teaching, one considers it and examines whether it is really rational, beneficial, and practical. And if it is satisfying at the intellectual level, one accepts it as true. Still this is not one's own insight, but only an intellectualization of the wisdom one has heard.

The third type of wisdom is that which arises out of one's own experience, out of personal realization of truth. This is the wisdom that one lives, real wisdom that will bring about a change in one's life by changing the very nature of the mind.

In worldly matters, experiential wisdom may not always be necessary or advisable. It is sufficient to accept the warnings of others that fire is dangerous, or to confirm the fact by deductive reasoning. It is foolhardy to insist on plunging oneself into fire before accepting that it burns. In Dhamma, however, the wisdom that comes of experience is essential, since only this enables us to become free from conditioning.

Wisdom acquired through listening to others and wisdom ac-

quired through intellectual investigation are helpful if they inspire
and guide us to advance to the third type of *paññā*, experiential
wisdom. But if we remain satisfied simply to accept received wisdom without questioning, it becomes a form of bondage, a barrier
to the attainment of experiential understanding. By the same to-
ken, if we remain content merely to contemplate truth, to investigate and understand it intellectually, but make no effort to experience it directly, then all our intellectual understanding becomes a
bondage instead of an aid to liberation.

Each one of us must live truth by direct experience, by the practice of *bhāvanā;* only this living experience will liberate the mind.
No one else's realization of truth will liberate us. Even the enlightenment of the Buddha could liberate only one person, Siddhattha
Gotama. At most, someone else's realization can act as an inspiration for others, offering guidelines for them to follow, but ultimately we each must do the work ourselves. As the Buddha said,

> You have to do your own work;
> those who have reached the goal will only show the way.[3]

Truth can be lived, can be experienced directly, only within oneself.
Whatever is outside is always at a distance from us. Only within
can we have actual, direct, living experience of reality.

Of the three types of wisdom, the first two are not peculiar to
the teaching of the Buddha. Both existed in India before him, and
even in his own time there were those who claimed to teach whatever he taught.[4] The unique contribution of the Buddha to the
world was a way to realize truth personally and thus to develop experiential wisdom, *bhāvanā-mayā paññā*. This way to achieve direct realization of truth is the technique of *vipassanā-bhāvanā*.

Vipassanā-bhāvanā

Vipassanā is often described as being a flash of insight, a sudden
intuition of truth. The description is correct, but in fact there is a
step-by-step method which meditators can use to advance to the
point that they are capable of such intuition. This method is *Vipassanā-bhāvanā*, the development of insight, commonly called Vipassana meditation.

The word *passanā* means "seeing," the ordinary sort of vision that we have with open eyes. *Vipassanā* means a special kind of vision: observation of the reality within oneself. This is achieved by taking as the object of attention one's own physical sensations. The technique is the systematic and dispassionate observation of sensations within oneself. This observation unfolds the entire reality of mind and body.

Why sensation? First because it is by sensations that we experience reality directly. Unless something comes into contact with the five physical senses or the mind, it does not exist for us. These are the gates through which we encounter the world, the bases for all experience. And whenever anything comes into contact with the six sensory bases, a sensation occurs. The Buddha described the process as follows: "If someone takes two sticks and rubs one against the other, then from the friction heat is generated, a spark is produced. In the same way, as the result of a contact to be experienced as pleasant, a pleasant sensation arises. As the result of a contact to be experienced as unpleasant, an unpleasant sensation arises. As the result of a contact to be experienced as neutral, a neutral sensation arises."[5]

The contact of an object with mind or body produces a spark of sensation. Thus sensation is the link through which we experience the world with all its phenomena, physical and mental. In order to develop experiential wisdom, we must become aware of what we actually experience; that is, we must develop awareness of sensations.

Further, physical sensations are closely related to the mind, and like the breath they offer a reflection of the present mental state. When mental objects—thoughts, ideas, imaginations, emotions, memories, hopes, fears—come into contact with the mind, sensations arise. Every thought, every emotion, every mental action is accompanied by a corresponding sensation within the body. Therefore by observing the physical sensations, we also observe the mind.

Sensation is indispensable in order to explore truth to the depths. Whatever we encounter in the world will evoke a sensation within the body. Sensation is the crossroads where mind and body meet. Although physical in nature, it is also one of the four mental processes (see Chapter Two). It arises within the body and is felt by the mind. In a dead body or inanimate matter, there can be no sensation, because mind is not present. If we are unaware of this experience, our investigation of reality remains incomplete and superficial. Just as to rid a garden of weeds one must be aware of the hidden roots and their vital function, similarly we must be aware of sensations, most of which usually remain hidden to us, if we are to understand our nature and deal with it properly.

Sensations occur at all times throughout the body. Every contact, mental or physical, produces a sensation. Every biochemical reaction gives rise to sensation. In ordinary life, the conscious mind lacks the focus necessary to be aware of all but the most intense of them, but once we have sharpened the mind by the practice of *ānāpāna-sati* and thus developed the faculty of awareness, we become capable of experiencing consciously the reality of every sensation within.

In the practice of awareness of respiration the effort is to observe natural breathing, without controlling or regulating it. Similarly, in the practice of *vipassanā-bhāvanā*, we simply observe bodily sensations. We move attention systematically throughout the physical structure from head to feet and feet to head, from one extremity to the other, but while doing so we do not search for a particular type of sensation, nor try to avoid sensations of another type. The effort is only to observe objectively, to be aware of whatever sensations manifest themselves throughout the body. They may be of any type: heat, cold, heaviness, lightness, itching, throbbing, contraction, expansion, pressure, pain, tingling, pulsation, vibration, or anything else. The meditator does not search for anything extraordinary but tries merely to observe ordinary physical sensations as they naturally occur.

Nor is any effort made to discover the cause of a sensation. It may arise from atmospheric conditions, because of the posture in which one sits, because of the effects of an old disease or weakness in the body, or even because of the food one has eaten. The reason is unimportant and beyond one's concern. The important thing is to be aware of the sensation that occurs at this moment in the part of the body where the attention is focused.

When we first begin this practice, we may be able to perceive sensations in some parts of the body and not in others. The faculty of awareness is not yet fully developed, so we only experience the intense sensations and not the finer, subtler ones. However, we continue giving attention to every part of the body in turn, moving the focus of awareness in systematic order, without allowing the attention to be drawn unduly by the more prominent sensations. Having practiced the training of concentration, we have developed the ability to fix the attention on an object of conscious choosing. Now we use this ability to move awareness to every part of the body in an orderly progression, neither jumping past a part where sensation is unclear to another part where it is prominent, nor lingering over some sensations, nor trying to avoid others. In this way, we gradually reach the point where we can experience sensations in every part of the body.

When one begins the practice of awareness of respiration, the breathing often will be rather heavy and irregular. Then it gradually calms and becomes progressively lighter, finer, subtler. Similarly, when beginning the practice of *vipassanā-bhāvanā,* one often experiences gross, intense, unpleasant sensations that seem to last for a long time. At the same time, strong emotions or long-forgotten thoughts and memories may arise, bringing with them mental or physical discomfort, even pain. The hindrances of craving, aversion, sluggishness, agitation, and doubt which impeded one's progress during the practice of awareness of breathing may now reappear and gain such strength that it is altogether impossible to maintain the awareness of sensation. Faced with this situation one has no alternative but to revert to the practice of awareness of respiration in order once again to calm and sharpen the mind.

Patiently, without any feeling of defeat, as meditators we work to re-establish concentration, understanding that all these difficulties are actually the results of our initial success. Some deeply buried conditioning has been stirred up and has started to appear at the conscious level. Gradually, with sustained effort but without any tension, the mind regains tranquility and one-pointedness. The strong thoughts or emotions pass away, and one can return to the awareness of sensations. And with repeated, continuous practice, the intense sensations tend to dissolve into more uniform, subtler ones and finally into mere vibrations, arising and falling with great rapidity.

But whether the sensations are pleasant or unpleasant, intense or subtle, uniform or varied is irrelevant in meditation. The task is simply to observe objectively. Whatever the discomforts of the unpleasant sensations, whatever the attractions of the pleasant ones, we do not stop our work, do not allow ourselves to become distracted or caught up in any sensation; our job is merely to observe ourselves with the same detachment as a scientist observing in a laboratory.

Impermanence, Egolessness, and Suffering

As we persevere in meditation, we soon realize one basic fact: our sensations are constantly changing. Every moment, in every part of the body, a sensation arises, and every sensation is an indication of a change. Every moment changes occur in every part of the body, electromagnetic and biochemical reactions. Every moment, even more rapidly, the mental processes change and are manifested in physical changes.

This is the reality of mind and matter: It is changing and impermanent—**anicca**. Every moment the subatomic particles of which the body is composed arise and pass away. Every moment the mental functions appear and disappear, one after another. Everything inside oneself, physical and mental, just as in the world outside, is changing every moment. Previously, we may have known that this was true; we may have understood it intellectually. Now, however, by the practice of *vipassanā-bhāvanā,* we experience the reality of impermanence directly within the framework of the body. The direct experience of the transitory sensations proves to us our ephemeral nature.

Every particle of the body, every process of the mind is in a state of constant flux. There is nothing that remains beyond a single moment, no hard core to which one can cling, nothing that one can call "I" or "mine." This "I" is really just a combination of processes that are always changing.

Thus the meditator comes to understand another basic reality: **anattā**—there is no real "I," no permanent self or ego. The ego to which one is so devoted is an illusion created by the combination of mental and physical processes, processes in constant flux. Having explored body and mind to the deepest level, one sees that there is no immutable core, no essence that remains independent of the processes, nothing that is exempt from the law of impermanence. There is only an impersonal phenomenon, changing beyond one's control.

Then another reality becomes clear. Any effort to hold on to something, saying "This is I, this is me, this is mine" is bound to make one unhappy, because sooner or later this something to which one clings passes away, or else this "I" passes away. Attachment to what is impermanent, transitory, illusory, and beyond one's control is suffering, **dukkha**. We understand all this not because someone tells us it is so, but because we experience it within, by observing sensations within the body.

Equanimity

Then how is one not to make oneself unhappy? How is one to live without suffering? By simply observing without reacting: Instead of trying to keep one experience and to avoid another, to pull this close, to push that away, one simply examines every phenomenon objectively, with equanimity, with a balanced mind.

This sounds simple enough, but what are we to do when we sit to meditate for an hour, and after ten minutes feel a pain in the knee? At once we start hating the pain, wanting the pain to go away. But it does not go away; instead, the more we hate it, the stronger it becomes. The physical pain becomes a mental pain, causing great anguish.

If we can learn for one moment just to observe the physical pain; if even temporarily we can emerge from the illusion that it is *our* pain, that *we* feel pain; if we can examine the sensation objectively like a doctor examining someone else's pain, then we see that the pain itself is changing. It does not remain forever; every moment it changes, passes away, starts again, changes again.

When we understand this by personal experience, we find that the pain can no longer overwhelm and control us. Perhaps it goes away quickly, perhaps not, but it does not matter. We do not suffer from the pain any more because we can observe it with detachment.

The Way to Liberation

By developing awareness and equanimity, one can liberate oneself from suffering. Suffering begins because of ignorance of one's own reality. In the darkness of this ignorance, the mind reacts to every sensation with liking and disliking, craving and aversion. Every such reaction creates suffering now and sets in motion a chain of events that will bring nothing but suffering in the future.

How can this chain of cause and effect be broken? Somehow, because of past actions taken in ignorance, life has begun, the flow of mind and matter has started. Should one then commit suicide? No, that will not solve the problem. At the moment of killing oneself the mind is full of misery, full of aversion. Whatever comes next will also be full of misery. Such an action cannot lead to happiness.

Life has started, and one cannot escape from it. Then should one destroy the six bases of sensory experience? One could pluck out the eyes, cut out the tongue, destroy the nose and ears. But how could one destroy the body? How could one destroy the mind? Again it would be suicide, which is useless.

Should one destroy the objects of each of the six bases, all the sights and sounds, and so on? This is not possible. The universe is full of countless objects; one could never destroy them all. Once the six sensory bases exist, it is impossible to prevent their contact with their respective objects. And as soon as contact occurs, there is bound to be a sensation.

But this is the point at which the chain can be broken. The crucial link occurs at the point of sensation. Every sensation gives rise to liking or disliking. These momentary, unconscious reactions of liking and disliking are immediately multiplied and intensified into great craving and aversion, into attachment, producing misery now and in the future. This becomes a blind habit which one repeats mechanically.

By the practice of *vipassanā-bhāvanā,* however, we develop awareness of every sensation. And we develop equanimity: We do not react. We examine the sensation dispassionately, without liking or disliking it, without craving, aversion, or attachment. Instead of giving rise to fresh reactions, every sensation now gives rise to nothing but wisdom, *paññā,* insight: "This is impermanent, bound to change, arising to pass away."

The chain has been broken, suffering has been stopped. There is no fresh reaction of craving or aversion, and therefore no cause from which sufferings can arise. The cause of suffering is the *kamma,* the mental deed, that is, the blind reaction of craving and aversion, the *sankhāra.* When the mind is aware of sensation but maintains equanimity, there is no such reaction, no cause that will produce suffering. We have stopped making suffering for ourselves.

The Buddha said,

> All *sankhāras* are impermanent.
> When you perceive this with true insight,
> then you become detached from suffering;
> this is the path of purification.[6]

Here the word *sankhāra* has a very wide meaning. A blind reaction of the mind is called *sankhāra,* but the result of that action, its fruit, is also known as *sankhāra;* like seed, like fruit. Everything that we encounter in life is ultimately the result of our own mental actions. Therefore in the widest sense, *sankhāra* means anything in this conditioned world, whatever has been created, formed, composed. Hence, "All created things are impermanent," whether mental or physical, everything in the universe. When one observes this truth with experiential wisdom through the practice of *vipassanā-bhāvanā,* then suffering disappears, because one turns away from the causes of suffering; that is, one gives up the habit of craving and aversion. This is the path of liberation.

The entire effort is to learn how not to react, how not to produce a new *sankhāra.* A sensation appears, and liking or disliking begins. This fleeting moment, if we are unaware of it, is repeated and intensified into craving and aversion, becoming a strong emotion that eventually overpowers the conscious mind. We become caught up in the emotion, and all our better judgment is swept aside. The result is that we find ourselves engaged in unwholesome speech and action, harming ourselves and others. We create misery for ourselves, suffering now and in the future, because of one moment of blind reaction.

But if we are aware at the point where the process of reaction begins—that is, if we are aware of the sensation—we can choose not to allow any reaction to occur or to intensify. We observe the sensation without reacting, neither liking nor disliking it. It has no chance to develop into craving or aversion, into powerful emotion that can overwhelm us; it simply arises and passes away. The mind remains balanced, peaceful. We are happy now, and we can anticipate happiness in the future, because we have not reacted.

This ability not to react is very valuable. When we are aware of the sensations within the body, and at the same time maintain equanimity, in those moments the mind is free. Perhaps at first these may be only a few moments in a meditation period, and the rest of the time the mind remains submerged in the old habit of reaction to sensations, the old round of craving, aversion, and misery. But with repeated practice those few brief moments will become seconds, will become minutes, until finally the old habit of reaction is broken, and the mind remains continuously at peace. This is how suffering can be stopped. This is how we can cease producing misery for ourselves.

Questions and Answers

QUESTION: *Why must we move our attention through the body in a certain order?*

S. N. GOENKA: Because you are working to explore the entire reality of mind and matter. To do this you must develop the ability to feel what is happening in every part of the body; no part should remain blank. And you must also develop the ability to observe the entire range of sensations. This is how the Buddha described the practice: "Everywhere within the limits of the body one experiences sensation, wherever there is life within the body."' If you allow the attention to move at random from one part to another, one sensation to another, naturally it will always be attracted to the areas in which there are stronger sensations. You will neglect certain parts of the body, and you will not learn how to observe subtler sensations. Your observation will remain partial, incomplete, superficial. Therefore it is essential always to move the attention in order.

How do we know that we are not creating sensations?

You can give yourself a test. If you are doubtful whether the sensations you feel are real, you can give yourself two or three commands, auto-suggestions. If you find that the sensations change according to your commands, then you know that they are not real. In that case you must throw away the entire experience and start again, observing respiration for some time. But if you find that you cannot control the sensations, that they do not change according to your will, then you must throw away the doubt and accept that the experience is real.

If these sensations are real, why don't we feel them in ordinary life?

You do, at the unconscious level. The conscious mind is unaware, but every moment the unconscious mind feels sensations in the body and reacts to them. This process happens twenty-four hours a day. But by practicing Vipassana, you break the barrier between conscious and unconscious. You become aware of everything that happens within the mental-physical structure, of everything that you experience.

Deliberately allowing ourselves to feel physical pain—this sounds like masochism.

It would be if you were asked just to experience pain. But instead you are asked to observe pain objectively. When you observe without reacting, automatically the mind starts to penetrate beyond the apparent reality of the pain to its subtle nature, which is nothing but vibrations arising and passing away every moment. And when you experience that subtle reality, the pain cannot master you. You are the master of yourself, you are free of the pain.

But surely the pain can be a signal that the blood supply has been cut off in a part of the body. Is it wise to ignore that signal?

Well, we have found that this exercise does not cause harm; if it did, we would not recommend it. Thousands of people have practiced this technique. I do not know of a single case where someone who was practicing properly injured himself. The common experience is that the body becomes more supple and flexible. The pain goes away when you learn to face it with a balanced mind.

Isn't it possible to practice Vipassana by observing at any of the six sense doors, for example, by observing the contact of the eye with vision and the ear with sound?

Certainly. But still that observation must involve awareness of sensation. Whenever a contact occurs at any of the six sense bases— eye, ear, nose, tongue, body, mind—a sensation is produced. If you remain unaware of it, you miss the point where reaction begins. In the case of most of the senses, contact may be only intermittent. At times your ears may hear a sound, at times not. However, at the deepest level there is a contact of mind and matter at every moment, continually giving rise to sensations. For this reason, observing sensations is the most accessible and vivid way to experience the fact of impermanence. You should master this before attempting to observe at the other sense doors.

If we should just accept and observe everything as it comes, how does progress come about?

Progress is measured according to whether you develop equanimity. You have no other real choice but equanimity, because you cannot change sensations, you cannot create sensations. Whatever comes, comes. It may be pleasant or unpleasant, of this type or that, but if you maintain equanimity, you are certainly progressing on the path. You are breaking the old mental habit of reaction.

That is in meditation, but how do you relate that to life?

When a problem arises in daily life, take a few moments to observe your sensations with a balanced mind. When the mind is calm and balanced, whatever decision you make will be a good one. When the mind is unbalanced, any decision you make will be a reaction. You must learn to change the pattern of life from negative reaction to positive action.

So if you are not angry or critical, but you see that something could be done differently, in a better way, then you go ahead and express yourself?

Yes. You must act. Life is for action; you should not become inactive. But the action should be performed with a balanced mind.

Today I was working to feel sensation in a part of the body that was dull, and as the sensation came up my mind gave me a kick; it felt just like hitting a home run. And I heard myself mentally yell "Good!" And then I thought, "Oh no, I don't want to react like that." But I wonder, back in the world, how can I go to a baseball game or a football game and not react?

You will *act!* Even in a football game you will act, not react, and you will find that you are really enjoying it. A pleasure accompanied by the tension of reaction is no real pleasure. When the reaction stops, the tension disappears, and you can really start to enjoy life.

So I can jump up and down and yell hooray?

Yes, with equanimity. You jump with equanimity.

What do I do if my team loses?

Then you smile and say "Be happy!" Be happy in every situation!

This seems to me the basic point.

Yes!

The Two Rings

A rich old man died leaving two sons. For some time the two continued living together in the traditional Indian way, in a single joint household, a joint family. Then they quarreled and decided to separate, dividing all the property between them. Everything was divided fifty-fifty, and thus they settled their affairs. But after the settlement had been made, a small packet was discovered which had been carefully hidden by their father. They opened the packet and found two rings inside, one set with a valuable diamond, and the other an ordinary silver ring worth only a few rupees.

Seeing the diamond, the elder brother developed greed in his mind, and he started explaining to the younger one, "To me it appears that this ring is not the earning of our father, but rather an heirloom from his forefathers. That is why he kept it separate from his other possessions. And since it has been kept for generations in our family, it should remain for future generations. Therefore I, being elder, shall keep it. You had better take the silver ring."

The younger brother smiled and said, "All right, be happy with the diamond ring, I'll be happy with the silver one." Both of them placed their rings on their fingers and went their ways.

The younger brother thought to himself, "It is easily understandable that my father kept the diamond ring; it is so valuable. But why did he keep this ordinary silver ring?" He examined the ring closely and found some words engraved on it: "This will also change." "Oh, this is the mantra of my father: 'This will also change!' " He replaced the ring on his finger.

Both brothers faced all the ups and downs of life. When spring came, the elder brother became highly elated, losing the balance of his mind. When autumn or winter came, he fell into deep depression, again losing his mental balance. He became tense, developing hypertension. Unable to sleep at night, he started using sleeping pills, tranquilizers, stronger drugs. Finally, he reached the stage where he required electric shock treatments. This was the brother with the diamond ring.

As for the younger brother with the silver ring, when spring came, he enjoyed it; he didn't try to run away from it. He enjoyed it, but looked at his ring and remembered, "This will also change." And when it changed, he could smile and say, "Well, I knew it was going to change. It has changed, so what!" When autumn or winter came, again he looked at his ring and remembered, "This will also change." He didn't start crying, knowing that this would also change. And yes, it also changed, it passed away. Of all the ups and downs, all the vicissitudes of life, he knew that nothing is eternal, that everything comes just to pass away. He did not lose the balance of his mind and he lived a peaceful, happy life.

This was the brother with the silver ring.

Chapter 8

AWARENESS AND EQUANIMITY

Awareness and equanimity—this is Vipassana meditation. When practiced together, they lead to liberation from suffering. If either is weak or lacking, it is not possible to progress on the path toward that goal. Both are essential, just as a bird requires two wings to fly or a cart needs two wheels to move. And they must be equally strong. If one wing of a bird is weak and the other powerful, it cannot fly properly. If one wheel of a cart is small and the other large, it will keep going around in circles. The meditator must develop both awareness and equanimity together in order to advance along the path.

We must become aware of the totality of mind and matter in their subtlest nature. For this purpose it is not enough merely to be mindful of superficial aspects of body and mind, such as physical movements or thoughts. We must develop awareness of sensations throughout the body and maintain equanimity toward them.

If we are aware but lack equanimity, then the more conscious we become of the sensations within and the more sensitive we become to them, the more likely we are to react, thereby increasing suffering. On the other hand, if we have equanimity, but know nothing about the sensations within, then this equanimity is only superficial, concealing reactions that are constantly going on unknown in the depths of the mind. Thus we seek to develop both awareness and equanimity at the deepest level. We seek to be conscious of everything that happens within and at the same time not to react to it, understanding that it will change.

This is true wisdom: the understanding of one's own nature, an understanding achieved by direct experience of truth deep within oneself. This is what the Buddha called **yathā-bhūta-ñāna-dassana,** the wisdom that arises on observing reality as it is. With this wisdom one can emerge from suffering. Every sensation that occurs will give rise only to the understanding of impermanence. All reactions cease, all *sankhāras* of craving and aversion. By learning how to observe reality objectively, one stops creating suffering for oneself.

The Stock of Past Reactions

Remaining aware and balanced is the way to stop producing new reactions, new sources of misery. But there is another dimension to our suffering which must also be dealt with. By ceasing to react from this moment forward, we may create no further cause of misery, but each one of us has a stock of conditioning, the sum total of our past reactions. Even if we add nothing new to the stock, the accumulated old *sankhāras* will still cause us suffering.

The word *sankhāra* may be translated as "formation," both the act of forming and that which is formed. Every reaction is the last step, the result in a sequence of mental processes, but it can also be the first step, the cause in a new mental sequence. Every *sankhāra* is both conditioned by the processes leading to it and also conditions the processes that follow.

The conditioning operates by influencing the second of the mental functions, perception (discussed in Chapter Two). Consciousness is basically undifferentiating, non-discriminating. Its purpose is merely to register that contact has occurred in mind or body. Perception, however, is discriminative. It draws on the store of past experiences in order to evaluate and categorize any new phenomenon. The past reactions become the points of reference by which we seek to understand a new experience; we judge and classify it in accordance with our past *sankhāras*.

In this way the old reactions of craving and aversion influence our perception of the present. Instead of seeing reality, we see "as through a glass darkly." Our perception of the world outside and of the world within is distorted and blurred by our past conditioning, our preferences and prejudices. In accordance with the distorted perception, an essentially neutral sensation immediately becomes pleasant or unpleasant. To this sensation we again react, creating fresh conditioning which distorts our perceptions further. In this way each reaction becomes the cause of future reactions, all conditioned by the past and conditioning the future in turn.

The dual function of *sankhāra* is shown in the Chain of Conditioned Arising (see pp. 48 & 49). The second link in the chain is *sankhāra*, which is the immediate precondition for the arising of consciousness, the first of the four mental processes. However, *sankhāra* is also last in the series of processes, following consciousness, perception, and sensation. In this form it reappears, later in the chain, after sensation, as the reaction of craving and aversion. Craving or aversion develop into attachment, which becomes the impetus for a new phase of mental and physical activity. Thus the process feeds on itself. Every *sankhāra* unleashes a chain of events that result in a new *sankhāra*, which unleashes a fresh chain of events in an endless repetition, a vicious circle. Every time that we react, we reinforce the mental habit of reaction. Every time that we develop craving or aversion, we strengthen the tendency of the mind to continue generating them. Once the mental pattern is established, we are caught in it.

For example, a man prevents someone from attaining a desired object. The thwarted person believes that man is very bad and dislikes him. The belief is based not on a consideration of the man's character, but only on the fact that he has frustrated the second person's desires. This belief is deeply impressed in the unconscious mind of the thwarted person. Every subsequent contact with that man is colored by it and gives rise to unpleasant sensation, which produces fresh aversion, which strengthens further the image. Even if the two meet after an interval of twenty years, the person who was thwarted long ago immediately thinks of that man as very bad and again feels dislike. The character of the first man may have changed totally in twenty years, but the second one judges him using the criterion of past experience. The reaction is not to the man himself, but to a belief about him based on the original blind reaction and therefore biased.

In another case, a man helps someone to achieve a desired object. The person who received assistance believes that man is very good, and likes him. The belief is based only on the fact that the man has helped to satisfy the second person's desires, not on careful consideration of his character. The positive belief is recorded in the unconscious and colors any subsequent contact with that man, giving rise to pleasant sensation, which results in stronger liking, which further strengthens the belief. No matter how many years pass before the two meet again, the same pattern repeats itself with each fresh contact. The second person reacts not to the man himself, but only to his belief about him, based on the original blind reaction.

In this way a *sankhāra* can give rise to fresh reaction, both immediately and in the distant future. And each subsequent reaction becomes the cause of still further reactions, which are bound to bring nothing but more misery. This is the process of repetition of reactions, of suffering. We assume that we are dealing with external reality when actually we are reacting to our sensations, which are conditioned by our perceptions, which are conditioned by our reactions. Even if from this moment we stop generating new *sankhāras,* still we have to reckon with the accumulated past ones. Because of this old stock, a tendency to react will remain and at any time may assert itself, generating new misery for us. So long as this old conditioning persists, we are not entirely free from suffering.

How can one eradicate the old reactions? To find the answer to this question it is necessary to understand more deeply the process of Vipassana meditation.

Eradicating Old Conditioning

In practicing Vipassana, our task is simply to observe sensations throughout the body. The cause of any particular sensation is beyond our concern; it is sufficient to understand that every sensation is an indication of an internal change. The change may be either mental or physical in origin; mind and body function interdependently and often cannot be differentiated. Whatever occurs at one level is likely to be reflected at the other.

At the physical level, as discussed in Chapter Two (pp. 25–26), the body is composed of subatomic particles—*kalāpas*—which every moment arise and pass away with great rapidity. As they do so, they manifest in an infinite variety of combinations the basic qualities of matter—mass, cohesion, temperature, and movement—producing within us the entire range of sensations.

There are four possible causes for the arising of *kalāpas*. The first is the food we eat; the second is the environment in which we live. But whatever occurs in the mind has an effect on the body and can be responsible for the arising of *kalāpas*. Hence particles may also arise because of a mental reaction occurring at the present moment, or because of a past reaction which influences the present mental state. In order to function, the body requires food. If one stops feeding the body, however, it will not collapse at once. It can continue to support itself, if necessary, for weeks by consuming the energy stored in its tissues. When all the stored energy is consumed, at last the body will collapse and die: the physical flow comes to an end.

In the same way the mind requires activity in order to maintain the flow of consciousness. This mental activity is *sankhāra*. According to the chain of conditioned arising, consciousness originates from reaction (see p. 48). Each mental reaction is responsible for giving impetus to the flow of consciousness. And while the body requires food only at intervals throughout the day, the mind requires constant fresh stimulation. Without it, the flow of consciousness cannot continue even for an instant. For example, at a given moment one generates aversion in the mind: in the next moment the consciousness that arises is the product of this aversion, and so on, moment after moment. One keeps repeating the reaction of aversion from one moment to the next, and keeps giving new input to the mind.

By practicing Vipassana, however, the meditator learns not to react. At a given moment, he creates no *sankhāra,* he gives no fresh stimulation to the mind. What happens then to the psychic flow? It does not stop at once. Instead, one or another of the accumulated past reactions will come to the surface of the mind in order to sustain the flow. A past conditioned response will arise and from this base consciousness continues for another moment. The conditioning will appear at the physical level by causing a particular type of *kalāpa* to arise, which one then experiences as sensation within the body. Perhaps a past *sankhāra* of aversion arises, manifesting itself as particles, which one experiences as an unpleasant burning sensation within the body. If one reacts to that sensation with disliking, fresh aversion is created. One has started giving fresh input to the flow of consciousness, and there is no opportunity for another of the stock of past reactions to rise to the conscious level.

However, if an unpleasant sensation occurs and one does not react, then no new *sankhāras* are created. The *sankhāra* that has arisen from the old stock passes away. In the next moment, another past *sankhāra* arises as sensation. Again, if one does not react, it passes away. In this way, by maintaining equanimity, we allow accumulated past reactions to arise at the surface of the mind, one after another, manifesting themselves as sensations. Gradually, by maintaining awareness and equanimity toward sensation, we eradicate the past conditioning.

So long as conditioning of aversion remains, the tendency of the unconscious mind will be to react with aversion when facing any unpleasant experience in life. So long as conditioning of craving remains, the mind will tend to react with craving in any pleasant situation. Vipassana works by eroding these conditioned responses. As we practice, we keep encountering pleasant and unpleasant sensations. By observing every sensation with equanimity, we gradually weaken and destroy the tendencies of craving and aversion. When the conditioned responses of a certain type are eradicated, one is free of that type of suffering. And when all conditioned responses have been eradicated one after another, the mind is totally liberated. One who well understood this process said,

> Impermanent truly are conditioned things,
> having the nature of arising and passing away.
> If they arise and are extinguished,
> their eradication brings true happiness.[1]

Every *sankhāra* arises and passes away, only in the next moment to arise again in endless repetition. If we develop wisdom and start observing objectively, the repetition stops and eradication begins. Layer after layer, the old *sankhāras* will arise and be eradicated, provided we do not react. As much as the *sankhāras* are eradicated, that much happiness we enjoy, the happiness of freedom from suffering. If all the past *sankhāras* are eradicated, we enjoy the limitless happiness of full liberation.

Vipassana meditation therefore is a kind of fasting of the spirit in order to eliminate past conditioning. Every moment for the whole of our lives we have generated reactions. Now, by remaining aware and balanced, we achieve a few moments in which we do not react, do not generate any *sankhāra*. Those few moments, no matter how brief, are very powerful; they set in motion the reverse process, the process of purification.

To trigger this process, we must literally do nothing; that is, we must simply refrain from any fresh reaction. Whatever might be the cause of the sensations we experience, we observe them with equanimity. The very act of generating awareness and equanimity will automatically eliminate old reactions, just as lighting a lamp will dispel the darkness from a room.

The Buddha once told a story about a man who had made great gifts of charity. But in concluding, the Buddha commented,

Even if he had performed the greatest charity, it would have been still more fruitful for him to take refuge with an accepting heart in the enlightened one, in the Dhamma, and in all saintly persons. And had he done so, it would have been still more fruitful for him to undertake with an accepting heart the five precepts. And had he done so, it would have been still more fruitful for him to cultivate good will toward all just for the time it takes to milk a cow. And had he done all of these, it would have been still more fruitful for him to develop the awareness of impermanence just for the time it takes to snap one's fingers.[2]

Perhaps the meditator is aware of the reality of sensations in the body only for a single moment, and does not react because he understands their transient nature. Even this brief moment will have a powerful effect. With patient, repeated, continuous practice, those few moments of equanimity will increase, and the moments of reaction will decrease. Gradually the mental habit of reacting will be broken and the old conditioning eradicated, until the time comes when the mind is freed of all reactions, past and present, liberated from all suffering.

Questions and Answers

QUESTION: *This afternoon I tried a new position in which it was easy to sit for longer without moving, keeping my back straight, but I could not feel many sensations. I wonder, will the sensations eventually come, or should I go back to the old position?*

S. N. GOENKA: Do not try to create sensations by deliberately choosing an uncomfortable position. If that were the proper way to practice, we would ask you to sit on a bed of nails! Such extremes will not help. Choose a comfortable position in which the body is upright, and let the sensations come naturally. Don't try to create them by force; just allow them to happen. They will come, because they are there. It may be that you were looking for sensations of the type you felt before, but there might be something else.

There were subtler sensations than before. In my first position it was hard to sit more than a short time without moving.

Then it is good that you have found a more suitable position. Now leave the sensations to nature. Perhaps some gross sensations have passed away and now you must deal with subtler ones, but the mind is not yet sharp enough to feel them. To make it sharper, work on the awareness of respiration for some time. This will improve your concentration and make it easy to feel subtle sensations.

I thought it was better if the sensations were gross, because that meant an old sankhāra *was coming up.*

Not necessarily. Certain impurities appear as very subtle sensations. Why crave for gross sensations? Whatever comes, gross or subtle, your job is to observe.

Should we try to identify which sensation is associated with which reaction?

That would be a meaningless waste of energy. It would be as if someone washing a dirty cloth stopped to check what caused each stain in the cloth. This would not help him to do his job, which is only to clean the cloth. For this purpose the important thing is to have a piece of laundry soap and to use it in the proper way. If one washes the cloth properly, all the dirt is removed. In the same way you have received the soap of Vipassana; now make use of it to remove all impurities from the mind. If you search for the causes of particular sensations, you are playing an intellectual game and you forget about *anicca,* about *anattā.* This intellectualizing cannot help you come out of suffering.

I am confused about who is observing and who or what is being observed.

No intellectual answer can satisfy you. You must investigate for yourself: "What is this 'I' who is doing all this? Who is this 'I'?" Keep on exploring, analyzing. See whether any 'I' comes up; if so, observe it. If nothing comes then accept, "Oh, this 'I' is an illusion!"

Aren't some types of mental conditioning positive? Why try to eradicate those?

Positive conditioning motivates us to work toward liberation from suffering. But when that goal is attained, all conditioning is left behind, positive and negative. It is just like using a raft to cross a river. Once the river is crossed, one does not continue on one's journey carrying the raft on one's head. The raft has served its purpose. Now there is no more need for it, and it must be left behind.[3] In the same way, one who is fully liberated has no need of conditioning. A person is liberated not because of positive conditioning, but because of purity of mind.

Why do we experience unpleasant sensations when we start practicing Vipassana, and why do pleasant sensations come later?

Vipassana works by eradicating the grossest impurities first. When you clean a floor, first you sweep together all the rubbish and pieces of dirt, and with each succeeding sweeping you gather finer and finer dust. So in the practice of Vipassana: First the gross impurities of the mind are eradicated and subtler ones remain which appear as pleasant sensations. But there is a danger of developing craving for these pleasant sensations. Therefore you must be careful not to take a pleasant sensory experience as the final goal. You must keep observing every sensation objectively in order to eradicate all conditioned reactions.

You said that we have our dirty linen, and we also have the soap to wash it. I feel today as if I almost ran out of soap! This morning my practice was very powerful, but in the afternoon I began to feel really hopeless and angry, and to think, "Oh, what's the use!" It was just as if when the meditation was strong, an enemy inside me—the ego perhaps—matched that strength and knocked me out. And then I felt I did not have the strength to fight it. Is there some way to sidestep so that I don't have to fight so hard, some clever way to do it?

Maintain equanimity; that is the smartest way! What you have experienced is quite natural. When the meditation seemed to you to be going well, the mind was balanced, and it penetrated deeply into the unconscious. As a result of that deep operation, a past reaction was shaken and came to the surface level of the mind, and in the next sitting you had to face that storm of negativity. In such a situation equanimity is essential, because otherwise the negativity will overpower you, and you cannot work. If equanimity seems weak, start practicing the awareness of respiration. When a big storm comes, you have to put down your anchor and wait until it passes away. The breath is your anchor. Work with it and the storm will pass. It is good that this negativity has come to the surface, because now you have the opportunity to clear it out. If you keep equanimity it will pass away easily.

Am I actually getting that much good out of the practice if I don't have pain?

If you are aware and balanced, then—pain or no pain—you are certainly progressing. It is not that you must feel pain in order to make progress on the path. If there is no pain, accept that there is no pain. You just observe what *is.*

Yesterday I had an experience in which my entire body felt as if it had dissolved. It felt like it was just a mass of vibrations everywhere.

Yes?

And when this happened, I remembered that when I was a child I had had a similar experience. All these years I have been looking for a way to come back to that experience. And then there it was again.

Yes?

So naturally I wanted the experience to continue, I wanted to prolong it. But it changed and passed away. And then I was working just to make it come back again, but it didn't come back. Instead, by this morning I had only gross sensations.

Yes?

And then I realized how unhappy I was making myself by trying to get that experience.

Yes?

And then I realized that in fact we aren't here to get any particular experience. Right?

Right.

That in fact we are here to learn to observe every experience without reacting. Right?

Right.

So what this meditation is really about is developing equanimity. Right?

Right!

Nothing But Seeing

There lived a recluse near where Bombay now stands, a very saintly man. All who met him revered him for his purity of mind, and many claimed that he must be fully liberated. Hearing himself described in such high terms, naturally this man began to wonder, "Perhaps I am in fact fully liberated." But being an honest person, he examined himself carefully and found that there were still traces of impurities in his mind. Surely as long as impurities remained, he could not have reached the stage of perfect saintliness. So he asked those who came to pay respects to him, "Is there not anyone else in the world today who is known to be fully liberated?"

"Oh yes sir," they replied, "there is the monk Gotama, called the Buddha, who lives in the city of Sāvatthi. He is known to be fully liberated, and he teaches the technique by which one can achieve liberation."

"I must go to this man," the recluse resolved. "I must learn from him the way to become fully liberated." So he started walking from Bombay across all of central India and came at last to Savatthi, which is in the modern-day state of Uttar Pradesh, in northern India. Having arrived in Sāvatthi he made his way to the meditation center of the Buddha, and asked where he might find him.

"He has gone out," one of the monks replied. "He has gone to beg for his meal in the city. Wait here and rest from your journey; he will return shortly."

"Oh no, I cannot wait. I have no time to wait! Show me which way he has gone and I shall follow."

"Well, if you insist, there is the road he took. If you like, you can try to find him along the way." Without wasting a moment the re-

cluse set off again, and came to the center of the city. There he saw
a monk going from house to house to beg for his food. The wonderful atmosphere of peace and harmony which surrounded this person convinced the recluse that he must be the Buddha, and asking
a passer-by he found that it was indeed so.

There in the middle of the street, the recluse approached the
Buddha, bowed down, and caught hold of his feet. "Sir," he said,
"I am told that you are fully liberated, and that you teach a way to
achieve liberation. Please teach this technique to me."

The Buddha said, "Yes, I teach such a technique, and I can
teach it to you. But this is not the proper time or place. Go and
wait for me at my meditation center. I'll soon return and teach you
the technique."

"Oh no sir, I cannot wait."

"What, not for half an hour?"

"No sir, I cannot wait! Who knows? In half an hour I may die.
In half an hour you may die. In half an hour all the confidence I
have in you may die, and then I shan't be able to learn this technique. Now, sir, is the time. Please teach me now!"

The Buddha looked at him and saw, "Yes, this man has little
time left; he will die in just a few minutes. He must be given
Dhamma here and now." And how to teach Dhamma while stand-
ing in the middle of the street? He spoke only a few words, but
those words contained the entire teaching: "In your seeing, there
should be only seeing; in your hearing nothing but hearing; in your
smelling, tasting, touching nothing but smelling, tasting, touching;
in your cognizing, nothing but cognizing." When contact occurs
through any of the six bases of sensory experience, there should be
no valuation, no conditioned perception. Once perception starts
evaluating any experience as good or bad, one sees the world in a
distorted way because of one's old blind reactions. In order to free
the mind from all conditioning, one must learn to stop evaluating
on the basis of past reactions and to be aware, without evaluating
and without reacting.

The recluse was a man of such pure mind that these few words
of guidance were enough for him. There by the side of the road, he
sat down and fixed his attention on the reality within. No valuation, no reaction; he simply observed the process of change within
himself. And within the few minutes left to him to live, he attained
the final goal, he became fully liberated.[4]

Chapter 9

THE GOAL

"Whatever has the nature of arising also has the nature of cessation."[1] The experience of this reality is the essence of the teaching of the Buddha. Mind and body are merely a bundle of processes that are constantly arising and passing away. Our suffering arises when we develop attachment to the processes, to what is in fact ephemeral and insubstantial. If we can realize directly the impermanent nature of these processes, our attachment to them passes away. This is the task that meditators undertake: to understand their own transient natures by observing the ever-changing sensations within. Whenever a sensation occurs they do not react, but allow it to arise and to pass away. By doing so they allow the old conditioning of the mind to come to the surface and pass away. When conditioning and attachment cease, suffering ceases, and we experience liberation. It is a long task requiring continual application. Benefits appear at every step along the way, but to attain them requires repeated effort. Only by working patiently, persistently, and continuously can the meditator advance toward the goal.

Penetration to Ultimate Truth

There are three stages in one's progress on the path. The first is simply learning about the technique, how it is done and why. The second is putting it into practice. The third is penetration, using the technique in order to pierce to the depths of one's reality and thereby to progress toward the final goal.

The Buddha did not deny the existence of the apparent world of shapes and forms, colors, tastes, smells, pains and pleasures, thoughts and emotions, of beings—oneself and others. He stated merely that this is not the *ultimate* reality. With ordinary vision, we perceive only the large-scale patterns into which more subtle phenomena organize themselves. Seeing only the patterns and not the underlying components, we are aware primarily of their differences, and therefore we draw distinctions, assign labels, form preferences and prejudices, and commence liking and disliking—the process that develops into craving and aversion.

In order to emerge from the habit of craving and aversion, it is necessary not only to have an overall vision, but to see things in depth, to perceive the underlying phenomena that compose apparent reality. This is precisely what the practice of Vipassana meditation allows us to do.

Any self-examination naturally begins with the most obvious aspects of ourselves: the different parts of the body, the various limbs and organs. Closer inspection will reveal that some parts of the body are solid, others are liquid, others are in motion or at rest. Perhaps we perceive the bodily temperature as distinct from the temperature of the surrounding atmosphere. All these observations may help to develop greater self-awareness, but they are still the results of examining apparent reality in a composed shape or form. Therefore distinctions persist, preferences and prejudices, craving and aversion.

As meditators we go further by practicing awareness of sensations within. These certainly reveal a subtler reality of which we were previously ignorant. At first we are aware of different types of sensations in different parts of the body, sensations that seem to arise, to remain for some time, and eventually to pass away. Although we have advanced beyond the superficial level, we are still observing the integrated patterns of apparent reality. For this reason we are not yet free from discriminations, from craving and aversion.

If we continue practicing diligently, sooner or later we arrive at a stage where the nature of the sensations changes. Now we are aware of a uniform type of subtle sensations throughout the body, arising and passing away with great rapidity. We have penetrated beyond the integrated patterns to perceive the underlying phenomena of which they are composed, the subatomic particles of which all matter is constituted. We experience directly the ephemeral nature of these particles, continually arising and vanishing. Now whatever we observe within, whether blood or bone, solid, liquid, or gaseous, whether ugly or beautiful, we perceive only as a mass of vibrations that cannot be differentiated. At last the process of drawing distinctions and assigning labels ceases. We have experienced within the framework of our own bodies the ultimate truth about matter: that it is constantly in flux, arising and passing away.

Similarly, the apparent reality of mental processes may be penetrated to a subtler level. For example, a moment of liking or disliking occurs, based on one's past conditioning. Next moment the mind repeats the reaction of liking or disliking, and reinforces it moment after moment until it develops into craving or aversion. We are aware only of the intensified reaction. With this superficial perception we begin to identify and discriminate between pleasant and unpleasant, good and bad, wanted and unwanted. But just as in the case of apparent material reality, so with intensified emotion: when we start to observe it by observing sensations within, it is bound to dissolve. As matter is nothing but subtle wavelets of subatomic particles, so strong emotion is merely the consolidated form of momentary likings and dislikings, momentary reactions to sensations. Once strong emotion dissolves into its subtler form, it no longer has any power to overwhelm.

From observing different consolidated sensations in different parts of the body, we proceed to awareness of subtler sensations of uniform nature, arising and vanishing constantly throughout the physical structure. Because of the great rapidity with which the sensations appear and disappear, they may be experienced as a flow of vibrations, a current moving through the body. Wherever we fix the attention within the physical structure, we are aware of nothing but arising and vanishing. Whenever a thought appears in the mind, we are aware of the accompanying physical sensations, arising and passing away. The apparent solidity of body and mind dissolves, and we experience the ultimate reality of matter, mind, and mental formations: nothing but vibrations, oscillations, arising and vanishing with great rapidity. As one who experienced this truth said,

> The entire world is ablaze,
> the entire world is going up in smoke.
> The entire world is burning,
> the entire world is vibrating.[2]

To reach this stage of dissolution (**bhanga**), the meditator need do nothing but develop awareness and equanimity. Just as a scientist can observe more minute phenomena by increasing the magnification of his microscope, so by developing awareness and equanimity one increases the ability to observe subtler realities within.

This experience, when it occurs, is certainly very pleasant. All the aches and pains have dissolved, all the areas without sensation have disappeared. One feels peaceful, happy, blissful. The Buddha described it as follows:

> Whenever one experiences
> the arising and passing away of the mental-physical processes,
> he enjoys bliss and delight.
> He attains the deathless, as realized by the wise.[3]

Bliss is bound to arise as one advances on the path, when the apparent solidity of mind and body has been dissolved. Delighting in the pleasant situation, we may think that it is the final goal. But it is only a way-station. From this point we proceed further to experience the ultimate truth *beyond* mind and matter, to attain total freedom from suffering.

The meaning of these words of the Buddha becomes very clear to us from our own practice in meditation. Penetrating from apparent to subtle reality, we begin to enjoy the flow of vibrations throughout the body. Then suddenly the flow is gone. Again we experience intense, unpleasant sensations in some parts, and perhaps no sensation in other parts. Again we experience intense emotion in the mind. If we start feeling aversion toward this new situation and craving for the flow to return, we have not understood Vipassana. We have turned it into a game in which the goal is to achieve pleasant experiences and to avoid or overcome unpleasant ones. This is the same game that we have played throughout life—the unending round of push and pull, of attraction and repulsion, which leads to nothing but misery.

As wisdom increases, however, we recognize that the recurrence of gross sensations, even after the experience of dissolution, indicates not regression but rather progress. We practice Vipassana not with the aim of experiencing any particular kind of sensation, but in order to free the mind of all conditioning. If we react to any sensation, we increase our suffering. If we remain balanced, we allow some of the conditioning to pass away and the sensation becomes a means to liberate us from suffering. By observing unpleasant sensations without reacting, we eradicate aversion. By observing pleasant sensations without reacting, we eradicate craving. By observing neutral sensations without reacting, we eradicate ignorance. Therefore no sensation, no experience is intrinsically good or bad. It is good if one remains balanced; it is bad if one loses equanimity.

With this understanding we use every sensation as a tool to eradicate conditioning. This is the stage known as **sankhara-upekkhā**, equanimity toward all conditioning, which leads step by step to the ultimate truth of liberation, *nibbāna*.

The Experience of Liberation

Liberation is possible. One can attain freedom from all conditioning, all suffering. The Buddha explained:

There is a sphere of experience that is beyond the entire field of matter, the entire field of mind, that is neither this world nor another world nor both, neither moon nor sun. This I call neither arising, nor passing away, nor abiding, neither dying nor rebirth. It is without support, without development, without foundation. This is the end of suffering.[4]

He also said,

There is an unborn, unbecome, uncreated, unconditioned. Were there not an unborn, unbecome, uncreated, unconditioned, no release would be known from the born, the become, the created, the conditioned. But since there is an unborn, unbecome, uncreated, unconditioned, therefore a release is known from the born, the become, the created, the conditioned.[5]

Nibbāna is not just a state one goes to after death; it is something to be experienced within oneself here and now. It is described in negative terms not because it is a negative experience but because we have no other way in which to describe it. Every language has words to deal with the entire range of physical and mental phenomena, but there are no words or concepts to describe something that is beyond mind and matter. It defies all categories, all distinctions. We can describe it only by saying what it is not.

In fact it is meaningless to try to describe *nibbāna*. Any description will only be confusing. Rather than discussing and arguing about it, the important thing is to experience it. "This noble truth of the cessation of suffering must be realized for oneself," the Buddha said.[6] When one has experienced *nibbāna,* only then is it real for him; then all arguments about it become irrelevant.

In order to experience the ultimate truth of liberation, it is necessary first to penetrate beyond apparent reality and to experience the dissolution of body and mind. The further one penetrates beyond apparent reality, the more one desists from craving and aversion, from attachments, and the nearer one approaches to ultimate truth. Working step by step, one naturally reaches a stage where the next step is the experience of *nibbāna*. There is no point in yearning for it, no reason to doubt that it will come. It must come to all who practice Dhamma correctly. When it will come, no one can say. This depends partly on the accumulation of conditioning within each person, partly on the amount of effort one expends to eradicate it. All one can do, all one need to do to attain the goal, is to continue observing each sensation without reacting.

We cannot determine when we shall experience the ultimate truth of *nibbāna,* but we can ensure that we keep progressing toward it. We can control the present state of mind. By maintaining equanimity no matter what occurs outside or within us, we achieve liberation in this moment. One who had attained the ultimate goal said, "Extinction of craving, extinction of aversion, extinction of ignorance—this is called *nibbāna*."[7] To the extent that the mind is freed of these, one experiences liberation.

Every moment in which we practice Vipassana properly, we can experience this liberation. After all, Dhamma by definition must give results here and now, not only in the future. We must experience its benefits at every step along the way, and every step must lead directly to the goal. The mind that at this moment is free from conditioning is a mind at peace. Each such moment brings us closer to total liberation.

We cannot strive to develop *nibbāna,* since *nibbāna* does not develop; it simply *is*. But we can strive to develop the quality that will lead us to *nibbāna,* the quality of equanimity. Every moment that we observe reality without reacting, we penetrate toward ultimate truth. The highest quality of the mind is equanimity based on full awareness of reality.

Real Happiness

Once the Buddha was asked to explain real happiness. He enumerated various wholesome actions which are productive of happiness, which are real blessings. All these blessings fall into two categories: performing actions that contribute to the welfare of others by fulfilling responsibilities to family and society, and performing actions that cleanse the mind. One's own good is inextricable from the good of others. And at last he said,

> When faced with all the ups and downs of life,
> still the mind remains unshaken,
> not lamenting, not generating defilements, always feeling secure;
> this is the greatest happiness.[8]

No matter what arises, whether within the microcosm of one's own mind and body or in the world outside, one is able to face it—not with tension, with barely suppressed craving and aversion—but with complete ease, with a smile that comes from the depths of the mind. In every situation, pleasant or unpleasant, wanted or unwanted, one has no anxiety, one feels totally secure, secure in the understanding of impermanence. This is the greatest blessing.

Knowing that you are your own master, that nothing can overpower you, that you can accept smilingly whatever life has to offer—this is perfect balance of the mind, this is true liberation. This is what can be attained here and now through the practice of Vipassana meditation. This real equanimity is not merely negative or passive aloofness. It is not the blind acquiescence or apathy of one who seeks escape from the problems of life, who tries to hide his head in the sand. Rather, true mental balance is based on full awareness of problems, awareness of all levels of reality.

The absence of craving or aversion does not imply an attitude of callous indifference, in which one enjoys one's own liberation but gives no thought to the suffering of others. On the contrary, real equanimity is properly called "holy indifference." It is a dynamic quality, an expression of purity of mind. When freed of the habit of blind reaction, the mind for the first time can take positive action which is creative, productive, and beneficial for oneself and for all others. Along with equanimity will arise the other qualities of a pure mind: good will, love that seeks the benefit of others without expecting anything in return; compassion for others in their failings and sufferings; sympathetic joy in their success and good fortune. These four qualities are the inevitable outcome of the practice of Vipassana.

Previously one always tried to keep whatever was good for oneself and pass anything unwanted on to others. Now one understands that one's own happiness cannot be achieved at the expense of others, that giving happiness to others brings happiness to oneself. Therefore one seeks to share whatever good one has with others. Having emerged from suffering and experienced the peace of liberation, one realizes that this is the greatest good. Thus one wishes that others may also experience this good, and find the way out of their suffering.

This is the logical conclusion of Vipassana meditation: **mettā-bhāvanā**, the development of good will toward others. Previously one may have paid lip service to such sentiments, but deep within the mind the old process of craving and aversion continued. Now to some extent the process of reaction has stopped, the old habit of egoism is gone, and good will naturally flows from the depths of the mind. With the entire force of a pure mind behind it, this good will can be very powerful in creating a peaceful and harmonious atmosphere for the benefit of all.

There are those who imagine that always remaining balanced means that one can no longer enjoy life in all its variety, as if a painter had a palette full of colors and chose to use nothing but gray, or as if one had a piano and chose to play nothing but middle C. This is a wrong understanding of equanimity. The fact is that the piano is out of tune and we do not know how to play it. Simply pounding the keys in the name of self-expression will only create discord. But if we learn how to tune the instrument and to play it properly, then we can make music. From the lowest to the highest note we use the full range of the keyboard, and every note that we play creates nothing but harmony, beauty.

The Buddha said that in cleansing the mind and attaining "wisdom brought to full perfection," one experiences "joy, bliss, tranquility, awareness, full understanding, real happiness."[9] With a balanced mind we can enjoy life more. When a pleasant situation occurs, we can savor it completely, having full and undistracted awareness of the present moment. But when the experience passes, we do not become distressed. We continue to smile, understanding that it was bound to change. Equally, when an unpleasant situation occurs, we do not become upset. Instead we understand it and by doing so perhaps we find a way to alter it. If that is not within our power, then we still remain peaceful, knowing full well that this experience is impermanent, bound to pass away. In this way, by keeping the mind free of tension, we can have a more enjoyable and productive life.

There is a story that in Burma people used to criticize the students of Sayagyi U Ba Khin, saying that they lacked the serious demeanor proper to those who practice Vipassana meditation. During a course, the critics admitted, they worked seriously, as they should, but afterward they always appeared happy and smiling. When the criticism came to the ears of Webu Sayadaw, one of the most highly respected monks in the country, he replied, "They smile because they *can* smile." Theirs was a smile not of attachment or ignorance, but of Dhamma. Someone who has cleansed the mind will not go about with a frown. When suffering is removed, naturally one smiles. When one learns the way to liberation, naturally one feels happy.

This smile from the heart expressing nothing but peace, equanimity and good will, a smile that remains bright in every situation, is real happiness. This is the goal of Dhamma.

Questions and Answers

QUESTION: *I wonder whether we can treat obsessive thoughts in the same way that we treat physical pain.*

S. N. GOENKA: Just accept the fact that there is obsessive thought or emotion in the mind. It is something that was deeply suppressed and now has appeared at the conscious level. Do not go into the details of it. Just accept emotion as emotion. And along with it, what sensation do you feel? There cannot be an emotion without a sensation at the physical level. Start observing that sensation.

Then do we look for the sensation related to that particular emotion?

Observe any sensation that occurs. You cannot find which sensation is related to the emotion, so never try to do that; it is indulging in a futile effort. At a time when there is emotion in the mind, whatever sensation you experience physically has a relation to that emotion. Just observe the sensations and understand, "These sensations are *anicca*. This emotion is also *anicca*. Let me see how long it lasts." You will find that you have cut the roots of the emotion and it passes away.

Would you say that emotion and sensation are the same?

They are two sides of the same coin. Emotion is mental and sensation is physical, but the two are interrelated. Actually every emotion, anything that arises in the mind, must arise along with a sensation in the body. This is the law of nature.

But emotion itself is a matter of the mind?

A matter of the mind, surely.

But the mind is also the whole body?

It is closely related to the entire body.

Consciousness is in all the atoms of the body?

Yes. That is why sensation related to a particular emotion can arise anywhere within the body. If you observe sensations throughout the body, you are certainly observing the sensation related to that emotion. And you come out of the emotion.

If we are sitting but not able to feel any sensation, is there still any benefit in the practice?

If you sit and observe respiration, it will calm and concentrate the mind, but unless you feel sensation, the process of cleansing cannot work at the deeper levels. In the depths of the mind, reactions start with sensation, which occurs constantly.

During daily life if we have a few moments, is it helpful to be still and observe sensations?

Yes. Even with open eyes, when you have no other work, you should be aware of the sensations within you.

How does a teacher recognize that a student has experienced nibbāna?

There are various ways to check at the time when someone is actually experiencing *nibbāna*. For this a teacher must be properly trained.

How can meditators know for themselves?

By the change that comes in their lives. People who have really experienced *nibbāna* become saintly and pure-minded. They no longer break the basic five precepts in any major way, and instead of concealing a mistake, they admit it openly and try hard not to repeat it. Clinging to rituals and ceremonies drops away, because they recognize them as only external forms, empty without the actual experience. They have unshakable confidence in the path that led them to liberation; they do not continue to search for other ways. And finally, the illusion of ego will be shattered in them. If people claim to have experienced *nibbāna* but their minds remain as impure and their actions as unhealthy as before, then something is wrong. Their way of life must show whether they have really experienced it.

It is not appropriate for a teacher to issue "certificates" to students—to announce that they have attained *nibbāna*. Otherwise it becomes an ego-building competition for teacher and for students. The students strive only to get a certificate, and the more certificates a teacher issues, the higher is his reputation. The experience of *nibbāna* becomes secondary, the certificate takes primary importance, and it all becomes a mad game. Pure Dhamma is only to help people, and the best help is to see that a student really experiences *nibbāna* and becomes liberated. The whole purpose of the teacher and the teaching is to help people genuinely, not to boost their egos. It is not a game.

How would you compare psychoanalysis and Vipassana?

In psychoanalysis you try to recall to consciousness past events that had a strong influence in conditioning the mind. Vipassana, on the other hand, will lead the meditator to the deepest level of the mind where conditioning actually begins. Every incident that one might try to recall in psychoanalysis has also registered a sensation at the physical level. By observing physical sensations throughout the body with equanimity, the meditator allows innumerable layers of conditioning to arise and pass away. He deals with the conditioning at its roots and can free himself from it quickly and easily.

What is true compassion?

It is the wish to serve people, to help them out of suffering. But it must be without attachment. If you start crying over the suffering of others, you only make yourself unhappy. This is not the path of Dhamma. If you have true compassion, then with all love you try to help others to the best of your ability. If you fail, you smile and try another way to help. You serve without worrying about the results of your service. This is real compassion, proceeding from a balanced mind.

Would you say that Vipassana is the only way to reach enlightenment?

Enlightenment is achieved by examining oneself and eliminating conditioning. And doing this is Vipassana, no matter what name you may call it. Some people have never even heard of Vipassana, and yet the process has started to work spontaneously in them. This seems to have happened in the case of a number of saintly people in India, judging from their own words. But because they did not learn the process step by step, they were unable to explain it clearly to others. Here you have the opportunity to learn a step-by-step method that will lead you to enlightenment.

Filling the Bottle of Oil

A mother sent her son with an empty bottle and a ten-rupee note to buy some oil from the nearby grocer's shop. The boy went and had the bottle filled, but as he was returning he fell down and dropped it. Before he could pick it up, half of the oil spilled out. Finding the bottle half empty, he came back to his mother crying, "Oh, I lost half the oil! I lost half the oil!" He was very unhappy.

The mother sent another son with another bottle and another ten-rupee note. He also had the bottle filled, and while returning fell down and dropped it. Again half of the oil spilled out. Picking up the bottle, he came back to his mother very happy: "Oh look, I saved half the oil! The bottle fell down and could have broken. The oil started spilling out; all of it might have been lost. But I saved half the oil!" Both came to the mother in the same position, with a bottle that was half empty, half full. One was crying for the empty half, one was happy with the filled part.

Then the mother sent another son with another bottle and a ten-rupee note. He also fell down while returning and dropped the bottle. Half of the oil spilled out. He picked up the bottle and, like the second boy, came to his mother very happy: "Mother, I saved half the oil!" But this boy was a Vipassana boy, full not only of optimism, but also of realism. He understood, "Well, half of the oil was saved, but half was also lost." And so he said to his mother, "Now I shall go to the market, work hard for the whole day, earn five rupees, and get this bottle filled. By evening, I will have it filled." This is Vipassana. No pessimism; instead, optimism, realism, and "workism"!

Chapter 10

THE ART OF LIVING

Of all our preconceptions about ourselves, the most basic is that there *is* a self. On this assumption we each give highest importance to the self, making it the center of our universe. We do this even though we can see without much difficulty that among all the countless worlds, this is only one; and among all the countless beings of our world, again this is only one. No matter how much we inflate the self, it still remains negligible when measured against the immensity of time and space. Our idea of the self is obviously mistaken. Nevertheless we dedicate our lives to seeking self-fulfillment, considering that to be the way to happiness. The thought of living in a different way seems unnatural or even threatening.

But anyone who has experienced the torture of self-consciousness knows what a great suffering it is. So long as we are preoccupied with our wants and fears, our identities, we are confined within the narrow prison of the self, cut off from the world, from life. Emerging from this self-obsession is truly a release from bondage, enabling us to step forth into the world, to be open to life, to others, to find real fulfillment. What is needed is not self-denial or self-repression, but liberation from our mistaken idea of self. And the way to this release is by realizing that what we call self is in fact ephemeral, a phenomenon in constant change.

Vipassana meditation is a way to gain this insight. So long as one has not personally experienced the transitory nature of body and mind, one is bound to remain trapped in egoism and therefore bound to suffer. But once the illusion of permanence is shattered, the illusion of "I" automatically disappears, and suffering fades away. For the Vipassana meditator, *anicca,* the realization of the ephemeral nature of the self and the world, is the key that opens the door to liberation.

The importance of understanding impermanence is a theme that runs like a common strand through all the teaching of the Buddha. He said,

> Better a single day of life
> seeing the reality of arising and passing away
> than a hundred years of existence
> remaining blind to it.[1]

He compared the awareness of impermanence to the farmer's plowshare, which cuts through all roots as he plows a field; to the topmost ridge of a roof, higher than all the beams that support it; to a mighty ruler holding sway over vassal princes; to the moon whose brightness dims the stars; to the rising sun dispelling all darkness from the sky.[2] The last words that he spoke at the end of his life were, "All *sankhāras*—all created things—are subject to decay. Practice diligently to realize this truth."[3]

The truth of *anicca* must not merely be accepted intellectually. It must not be accepted only out of emotion or devotion. Each of us must experience the reality of *anicca* within ourselves. The direct understanding of impermanence and, along with it, of the illusory nature of the ego and of suffering, constitutes true insight which leads to liberation. This is right understanding.

The meditator experiences this liberating wisdom as the culmination of the practice of *sīla, samādhi,* and *paññā.* Unless one undertakes the three trainings, unless one takes every step along the path, one cannot arrive at real insight and freedom from suffering. But even before beginning the practice one must have some wisdom, perhaps only an intellectual recognition of the truth of suffering. Without such understanding, no matter how superficial, the thought of working to free oneself from suffering would never arise in the mind. "Right understanding comes first," the Buddha said.[4]

Thus the first steps of the Noble Eightfold Path are in fact right understanding and right thought. We must see the problem and decide to deal with it. Only then is it possible to undertake the actual practice of Dhamma. We begin to implement the path with training in morality, following the precepts to regulate our actions. With the training of concentration we begin to deal with the mind, developing *samādhi* by awareness of respiration. And by observing sensations throughout the body, we develop experiential wisdom which frees the mind of conditioning.

And now, when real understanding arises from one's own experience, again right understanding becomes the first step along the path. By realizing one's ever-changing nature through the practice of Vipassana, the meditator frees the mind of craving, aversion, and ignorance. With such a pure mind it is impossible to even think of harming others. Instead one's thoughts are filled only with good will and compassion toward all. In speech, action, and livelihood, one lives a blameless life, serene and peaceful. And with the tranquility resulting from the practice of morality, it becomes easier to develop concentration. And the stronger the concentration, the more penetrating one's wisdom will be. Thus the path is an ascending spiral leading to liberation. Each of the three trainings supports the others, like the three legs of a tripod. The legs must all be present and of equal length or the tripod cannot stand. Similarly, the meditator must practice *sīla, samādhi,* and *paññā* together to develop equally all facets of the path. The Buddha said,

> From right understanding proceeds right thought;
> from right thought proceeds right speech;
> from right speech proceeds right action;
> from right action proceeds right livelihood;
> from right livelihood proceeds right effort;
> from right effort proceeds right awareness;
> from right awareness proceeds right concentration;
> from right concentration proceeds right wisdom;
> from right wisdom proceeds right liberation.[5]

Vipassana meditation also has profound practical value here and now. In daily life innumerable situations arise that threaten the equanimity of the mind. Unexpected difficulties occur; unexpectedly others oppose us. After all, simply learning Vipassana is not a guarantee that we shall have no further problems, any more than learning to pilot a ship means that one will have only smooth voyages. Storms are bound to come; problems are bound to arise. Trying to escape from them is futile and self-defeating. Instead, the proper course is to use whatever training one has to ride out the storm.

In order to do so, first we must understand the true nature of the problem. Ignorance leads us to blame the external event or person, to regard that as the source of the difficulty, and to direct all our energy toward changing the external situation. But practice of Vipassana will bring the realization that no one but ourselves is responsible for our happiness or unhappiness. The problem lies in the habit of blind reaction. Therefore we ought to give attention to the inner storm of conditioned reactions of the mind. Simply resolving not to react will not work. So long as conditioning remains in the unconscious, sooner or later it is bound to arise and overpower the mind, all resolutions to the contrary notwithstanding. The only real solution is to learn to observe and change ourselves.

This much is easy enough to understand, but to implement it is more difficult. The question remains, how is one to observe oneself? A negative reaction has started in the mind—anger, fear, or hatred. Before one can remember to observe it, one is overwhelmed by it and speaks or acts negatively in turn. Later, after the damage is done, one recognizes the mistake and repents, but the next time repeats the same behavior.

Or, suppose that—realizing a reaction of anger has started—one actually tries to observe it. As soon as he tries, the person or situation one is angry at comes to mind. Dwelling on this intensifies the anger. Thus to observe emotion dissociated from any cause or circumstance is far beyond the ability of most.

But by investigating the ultimate reality of mind and matter, the Buddha discovered that whenever a reaction arises in the mind, two types of changes occur at the physical level. One of them is readily apparent: the breath becomes slightly rough. The other is more subtle in nature: a biochemical reaction, a sensation, takes place in the body. With proper training a person of average intelligence can easily develop the ability to observe respiration and sensation. This allows us to use changes in the breath and the sensations as warnings, to alert us to a negative reaction long before it can gather dangerous strength. And if we then continue observing respiration and sensation, we easily emerge from the negativity.

Of course the habit of reaction is deeply ingrained and cannot be removed all at once. However, in daily life, as we perfect our practice of Vipassana meditation, we notice at least a few occasions when instead of reacting involuntarily, we simply observe ourselves. Gradually the moments of observation increase and the moments of reaction become infrequent. Even if we do react negatively, the period and intensity of the reaction diminish. Eventually, even in the most provocative situations, we are able to observe respiration and sensation and to remain balanced and calm.

With this balance, this equanimity at the deepest level of the mind, one becomes capable for the first time of real action—and real action is always positive and creative. Instead of automatically responding in kind to the negativity of others, for example, we can select the response that is most beneficial. When confronted by someone burning with anger, an ignorant person himself becomes angry, and the result is a quarrel that causes unhappiness for both. But if we remain calm and balanced, we can help that person to emerge from anger and to deal constructively with the problem.

Observing our sensations teaches us that whenever we are overwhelmed by negativity, we suffer. Therefore, whenever we see others reacting negatively, we understand that they are suffering. With this understanding we can feel compassion for them and can act to help them free themselves of misery, not make them more miserable. We remain peaceful and happy and help others to be peaceful and happy.

Developing awareness and equanimity does not make us impassive and inert like vegetables, allowing the world to do what it likes with us. Nor do we become indifferent to the suffering of others while remaining absorbed in the pursuit of inner peace. Dhamma teaches us to take responsibility for our own welfare as well as for the welfare of others. We perform whatever actions are needed to help others, but always keeping balance of mind. Seeing a child sinking in quicksand, a foolish person becomes upset, jumps in after the child, and himself is caught. A wise person, remaining calm and balanced, finds a branch with which he can reach the child and drag him to safety. Jumping after others into the quicksand of craving and aversion will not help anyone. We must bring others to the firm ground of mental balance.

Many times in life strong action is necessary. For example, we may have tried to explain in mild, polite language to someone that he is making a mistake, but the person ignores the advice, being unable to understand anything except firm words and actions. Therefore one takes whatever firm action is required. Before acting, however, we must examine ourselves to see whether the mind is balanced, and whether we have only love and compassion for the person who is misbehaving. If so, the action will be helpful; if not, it will not really help anyone. If we act from love and compassion we cannot go wrong.

When we see a strong person attacking a weaker one, we have a responsibility to try to stop this unwholesome action. Any reasonable person will try to do so, although probably out of pity for the victim and anger toward the aggressor. Vipassana meditators will have equal compassion for both, knowing that the victim must be protected from harm, and the aggressor from harming himself by his unwholesome actions.

Examining one's mind before taking any strong action is extremely important; it is not sufficient merely to justify the action in retrospect. If we ourselves are not experiencing peace and harmony within, we cannot foster peace and harmony in anyone else. As Vipassana meditators we learn to practice committed detachment, to be both compassionate and dispassionate. We work for the good of all by working to develop awareness and equanimity. If we do nothing else but refrain from adding to the sum total of tensions in the world, we have performed a wholesome deed. But in truth the act of equanimity is loud by its very silence, with far-reaching reverberations that are bound to have a positive influence on many.

After all, mental negativity—our own and others'—is the root cause of the sufferings of the world. When the mind has become pure, the infinite range of life opens before us, and we can enjoy and share with others real happiness.

Questions and Answers

QUESTION: *May we tell others about the meditation?*

S. N. GOENKA: Certainly. There is no secrecy in Dhamma. You may tell anyone about what you have done here. But guiding people to practice is something totally different, which should not be done at this stage. Wait until you are firmly established in the technique and trained to guide others. If someone whom you tell about Vipassana is interested in practicing it, advise that person to come to a course. At least the first experience of Vipassana must be in an organized ten-day course, under the guidance of a qualified teacher. After that one can practice on one's own.

I practice yoga. How can I integrate this with Vipassana?

Here at a course, yoga is not permitted because it will disturb others by drawing their attention. But after you return home, you may practice both Vipassana and yoga—that is, the physical exercises of yogic postures and breath control. Yoga is very beneficial for physical health. You may even combine it with Vipassana. For example, you assume a posture and then observe sensations throughout the body; this will give still greater benefit than the practice of yoga alone. But the yogic meditation techniques using mantra and visualization are totally opposed to Vipassana. Do not mix them with this technique.

How about the different yogic breathing exercises?

They are helpful as physical exercise, but do not mix these techniques with *ānāpāna*. In *ānāpāna* you must observe natural breath as it is, without controlling it. Practice breath control as a physical exercise, and practice *ānāpāna* for meditation.

Am I—is not this bubble—becoming attached to enlightenment?

If so, you are running in the opposite direction from it. You can never experience enlightenment so long as you have attachments. Simply understand what enlightenment is. Then keep on observing the reality of this moment, and let enlightenment come. If it does not come, don't be upset. You just do your job and leave the result to Dhamma. If you work in this way, you are not attached to enlightenment and it will certainly come.

Then I meditate just to do my work?

Yes. It is your responsibility to cleanse your own mind. Take it as a responsibility, but do it without attachment.

It's not to achieve anything?

No. Whatever comes will come by itself. Let it happen naturally.

What is your feeling about teaching Dhamma to children?

The best time for that is before birth. During pregnancy the mother should practice Vipassana, so that the child also receives it and is born a Dhamma child. But if you already have children, you can still share Dhamma with them. For example, as the conclusion of your practice of Vipassana you have learned the technique of *mettā-bhāvanā*, sharing your peace and harmony with others. If your children are very young, direct your *mettā* to them after every meditation and at their bedtime; in this way they also benefit from your practice of Dhamma. And when they are older, explain a little about Dhamma to them in a way that they can understand and accept. If they can understand a little more, then teach them to practice *ānāpāna* for a few minutes. Don't pressure the children in any way. Just let them sit with you, observe their breath for a few minutes, and then go and play. The meditation will be like play for them; they will enjoy doing it. And most important is that you must live a healthy Dhamma life yourself, you must set a good example for your children. In your home you must establish a peaceful and harmonious atmosphere which will help them grow into healthy and happy people. This is the best thing you can do for your children.

Thank you very much for the wonderful Dhamma.

Thank Dhamma! Dhamma is great. I am only a vehicle. And also thank yourself. You worked hard, so you grasped the technique. A teacher keeps talking, talking, but if you do not work, you don't get anything. Be happy, and work hard, work hard!

The Striking of the Clock

I feel very fortunate that I was born in Burma, the land of Dhamma, where this wonderful technique was preserved through the centuries in its original form. About one hundred years ago my grandfather came from India and settled there, and so I was born in that country. And I feel very fortunate that I was born into a family of businessmen, and that from my teens I started working to gain money. Amassing money was my chief purpose in life. I am fortunate that from an early age I succeeded in earning a lot of money. If I had not myself known the life of riches, I would not have had the personal experience of the hollowness of such an existence. And had I not experienced this, some thought might always have lingered in a corner of my mind that true happiness lies in wealth. When people become rich, they are given special status and high positions in society. They become officers of many different organizations. From my early twenties I began this madness of seeking social prestige. And naturally all these tensions in my life gave rise to a psychosomatic disease, severe migraine headaches. Every fortnight I suffered an attack of this disease, for which there was no cure. I feel very fortunate that I developed this disease.

Even the best doctors in Burma could not cure my sickness. The only treatment that they had to offer was an injection of morphine to relieve an attack. Every fortnight I required an injection of morphine, and then I faced its after-effects: nausea, vomiting, misery.

After a few years of this affliction the doctors began to warn me, "Now you are taking morphine to relieve the attacks of your disease, but if you continue, soon you will become addicted to morphine, and you will have to take it every day." I was shocked at the prospect; life would be horrible. The doctors advised, "You often travel abroad on business; for once make a trip for the sake of your health.

We have no cure for your disease, and neither, we know, have doctors in other countries. But perhaps they have some other painkiller to relieve your attacks, which would free you from the danger of morphine dependence." Heeding their advice I traveled to Switzerland, Germany, England, America, and Japan. I was treated by the best doctors of these countries. And I am very fortunate that all of them failed. I returned home worse than when I had left.

After my return from this unsuccessful trip, a kind friend came and suggested to me, "Why not try one of these ten-day courses in Vipassana meditation? They are conducted by U Ba Khin, a very saintly man, a government officer, a family man like yourself. To me it seems that the basis of your disease is actually mental, and here is a technique that is said to free the mind of tensions. Perhaps by practicing it you can cure yourself of the disease." Having failed everywhere else I decided at least to go to meet this teacher of meditation. After all, I had nothing to lose.

I went to his meditation center and talked with this extraordinary man. Deeply impressed by the calm and peaceful atmosphere of the place and by his own peaceful presence, I said, "Sir, I want to join one of your courses. Will you please accept me?"

"Certainly, this technique is for one and all. You are welcome to join a course."

I continued, "For a number of years I have suffered from an incurable disease, severe migraine headaches. I hope that by this technique I may be cured of the disease."

"No," he suddenly said, "don't come to me. You may not join a course." I could not understand how I had offended him; but then with compassion he explained, "The purpose of Dhamma is not to cure physical diseases. If that is what you seek, you had better go to a hospital. The purpose of Dhamma is to cure all the miseries of life. This disease of yours is really a very minor part of your suffering. It will pass away, but only as a by-product in the process of mental purification. If you make the by-product your primary goal, then you devalue Dhamma. Come not for physical cures, but to liberate the mind."

He had convinced me. "Yes, sir," I said, "now I understand. I shall come only for the purification of my mind. Whether or not my disease may be cured, I should like to experience the peace that I see here." And giving him my promise, I returned home.

But still I postponed joining a course. Being born in a staunch, conservative Hindu family, from my childhood I had learned to recite the verse, "Better to die in your own religion, your own *dharma*;* never go to another religion." I said to myself, "Look, this is another religion, Buddhism. And these people are atheists, they don't believe in God or in the existence of a soul!" (As if simply believing in God or in the soul will solve all our problems!) "If I become an atheist, then what will happen to me? Oh no, I had better die in my own religion, I will never go near them."

For months I hesitated in this way. But I am very fortunate that at last I decided to give this technique a try, to see what would happen. I joined the next course and passed through the ten days. I am very fortunate that I benefited greatly. Now I could understand one's own *dharma,* one's own path, and the *dharma* of others. The *dharma* of human beings is one's own *dharma.* Only a human being has the ability to observe himself in order to come out of suffering. No lower creature has this faculty. Observing the reality within oneself is the *dharma* of human beings. If we do not make use of this ability, then we live the life of lower beings, we waste our lives, which is certainly dangerous.

I had always considered myself to be a very religious person. After all, I performed all the necessary religious duties, I followed the rules of morality, and I gave a lot to charity. And if I was not in fact a religious person, then why had I been made the head of so many religious organizations? Certainly, I thought, I must be very religious. But no matter how much charity or service I had given, no matter how careful I had been of my speech and actions, still when I started observing the dark chamber of the mind within, I found it to be full of snakes and scorpions and centipedes, because of which I had had to endure so much suffering. Now, as the impurities were gradually eradicated, I began to enjoy real peace. I realized how fortunate I was to receive this wonderful technique, the jewel of the Dhamma.

For fourteen years I was very fortunate to be able to practice this technique in Burma under the close guidance of my teacher.

---

*There is a play here on the various meanings of the word *dhamma,* or *dharma* in Sanskrit and modern Hindi. In India today, the word is given a narrow, sectarian meaning, which is here contrasted with its much wider ancient meaning of "nature."

Of course I fulfilled all my worldly responsibilities as a family man, and at the same time, every morning and evening, I continued meditating, every weekend I went to the center of my teacher, and every year I undertook a retreat of ten days or longer.

In early 1969 I had to make a trip to India. My parents had gone there a few years earlier and my mother had developed a nervous disease which I knew could be cured by the practice of Vipassana. But there was no one in India who could teach her. The technique of Vipassana had long been lost in that country, the land of its origin. Even the name had been forgotten. I am grateful to the government of Burma for allowing me to go to India; in those days they did not commonly permit their citizens to travel abroad. I am grateful to the government of India for allowing me to come to their country. In July of 1969, the first course was held in Bombay, in which my parents and twelve others participated. I am fortunate that I was able to serve my parents. By teaching them Dhamma I was able to repay my deep debt of gratitude to them.

Having fulfilled my purpose in coming to India, I was ready to return home to Burma. But I found that those who had participated in the course started pressing me to give another, and another. They wanted courses for their fathers, mothers, wives, husbands, children, and friends. So then the second course was held, and the third, and the fourth, and in this way the teaching of Dhamma began to spread.

In 1971, while I was giving a course in Bodh Gaya, I received a cable from Rangoon announcing that my teacher had passed away. Of course the news was shocking, being completely unexpected, and certainly it was very saddening. But with the help of the Dhamma he had given me, my mind remained balanced.

Now I had to decide how to pay back my debt of gratitude to this saintly person, Sayagyi U Ba Khin. My parents had given me birth as a human being, but one still enclosed in the shell of ignorance. It was only with the help of this wonderful person that I was able to break the shell, to discover truth by observing the reality within. And not only that, but for fourteen years he had strengthened and nurtured me in Dhamma. How could I repay the debt of gratitude to my Dhamma father? The only way that I could see was to practice what he had taught, to live the life of Dhamma; this is the proper way to honor him. And with as much purity of mind, as much love and compassion as I could develop, I resolved to devote the rest of my life to serving others, since this is what he wished me to do.

He often used to refer to the traditional belief in Burma that twenty-five centuries after the time of the Buddha, the Dhamma would return to the country of its origin, from there to spread around the world. It was his wish to help this prediction come to pass by going to India and teaching Vipassana meditation there. "Twenty-five centuries are over," he used to say; "the clock of Vipassana has struck!" Unfortunately, political conditions in his later years did not allow him to travel abroad. When I received permission to go to India in 1969, he was deeply pleased and told me, "Goenka, you are not going; I am going!"

At first I thought that this prediction was merely a sectarian belief. After all, why should something special happen after twenty-five centuries if it could not happen sooner? But when I came to India I was amazed to find that, although I did not know even one hundred people in that vast country, thousands started coming to courses, from every background, from every religion, from every community. Not only Indians, but thousands started coming from many different countries.

It became clear that nothing happens without a cause. No one comes to a course accidentally. Some perhaps have performed a wholesome act in the past, as a result of which they now have the opportunity to receive the seed of Dhamma. Others have already received the seed, and now they have come to help it grow. Whether you have come to get the seed or to develop the seed that you already have, keep growing in Dhamma for your own good, for your own benefit, for your own liberation, and you will find how it starts helping others too. Dhamma is beneficial for one and all.

May suffering people everywhere find this path of peace. May they all be released from their misery, their shackles, their bondage. May they free their minds of all defilements, all impurities.

May all beings throughout the universe be happy.

May all beings be peaceful.

May all beings be liberated.

THE IMPORTANCE OF *VEDANĀ*
IN THE TEACHING OF
THE BUDDHA

The teaching of the Buddha is a system for developing self-knowledge as a means to self-transformation. By attaining an experiential understanding of the reality of our own nature, we can eliminate the misapprehensions that cause us to act wrongly and to make ourselves unhappy. We learn to act in accordance with reality and therefore to lead productive, useful, happy lives.

In the **Satipaṭṭhāna Sutta**, the "Discourse on the Establishing of Awareness," the Buddha presented a practical method for developing self-knowledge through self-observation. This technique is Vipassana meditation.

Any attempt to observe the truth about oneself immediately reveals that what one calls "oneself" has two aspects, physical and psychic, body and mind. We must learn to observe both. But how can we actually experience the reality of body and mind? Accepting the explanations of others is not sufficient, nor is depending on merely intellectual knowledge. Both may guide us in the work of self-exploration, but each of us must explore and experience reality directly within ourselves.

We each experience the reality of the body by feeling it, by means of the physical sensations that arise within it. With eyes closed we know that we have hands, or any of the other parts of the body, because we can feel them. As a book has external form and internal content, the physical structure has an external, objective reality—the body (**kāya**)—and an internal, subjective reality of sensation (*vedanā*). We digest a book by reading all the words in it;

we experience the body by feeling sensations. Without awareness of sensations there can be no direct knowledge of the physical structure. The two are inseparable.

Similarly, the psychic structure can be analyzed into form and content: the mind (**citta**) and whatever arises in the mind (*dhamma*)—any thought, emotion, memory, hope, fear, any mental event. As body and sensation cannot be experienced separately, so one cannot observe the mind apart from the contents of the mind. But mind and matter are also closely interrelated. Whatever occurs in one is reflected in the other. This was a key discovery of the Buddha, of crucial significance in his teaching. As he expressed it, "Whatever arises in the mind is accompanied by sensation."[1] Therefore observation of sensation offers a means to examine the totality of one's being, physical as well as mental.

These four dimensions of reality are common to every human being: the physical aspects of body and sensation, the psychic aspects of mind and its content. They provide the four divisions of the *Satipaṭṭhāna Sutta,* the four avenues for the establishing of awareness, the four vantage points for observing the human phenomenon. If the investigation is to be complete, every facet must be experienced. And all four can be experienced by observing *vedanā*.

For this reason the Buddha specially stressed the importance of awareness of *vedanā*. In the *Brahmajāla Sutta,* one of his most important discourses, he said, "The enlightened one has become liberated and freed from all attachments by seeing as they really are the arising and passing away of sensations, the relishing of them, the danger of them, the release from them."[2] Awareness of *vedanā,* he stated, is a prerequisite for the understanding of the Four Noble Truths: "To the person who experiences sensation I show the way to realize what is suffering, its origin, its cessation, and the path leading to its cessation."[3]

What exactly is *vedanā?* The Buddha described it in various ways. He included *vedanā* among the four processes that compose the mind (see Chapter Two). However, when defining it more precisely he spoke of *vedanā* as having both mental and physical aspects.[4] Matter alone cannot feel anything if the mind is not present; in a dead body, for example, there are no sensations. It is the mind that feels, but what it feels has an inextricable physical element.

This physical element is of central importance in practicing the teaching of the Buddha. The purpose of the practice is to develop in us the ability to deal with all the vicissitudes of life in a balanced way. We learn to do so in meditation by observing with equanimity whatever happens within ourselves. With this equanimity, we can break the habit of blind reaction, and instead can choose the most beneficial course of action in any situation.

Whatever we experience in life is encountered through the six gates of perception, the five physical senses and the mind. And according to the Chain of Conditioned Arising, as soon as a contact occurs at any of these six gates, as soon as we encounter any phenomenon, physical or mental, a sensation is produced (see above, p. 49). If we do not give attention to what happens in the body, we remain unaware, at the conscious level, of the sensation. In the darkness of ignorance an unconscious reaction begins toward the sensation, a momentary liking or disliking, which develops into craving or aversion. This reaction is repeated and intensified innumerable times before it impinges on the conscious mind. If meditators give importance only to what happens in the conscious mind, they become aware of the process after the reaction has occurred and gathered dangerous strength, sufficient to overwhelm them. They allow the spark of sensation to ignite a raging fire before trying to extinguish it, needlessly making difficulties for themselves. But if they learn to observe the sensations within the body objectively, they permit each spark to burn itself out without starting a conflagration. By giving importance to the physical aspect, they become aware of *vedanā* as soon as it arises, and can prevent any reactions from occurring.

The physical aspect of *vedanā* is particularly important because it offers vivid, tangible experience of the reality of impermanence within ourselves. Change occurs at every moment within us, manifesting itself in the play of sensations. It is at this level that impermanence must be experienced. Observation of the constantly changing sensations permits the realization of one's own ephemeral nature. This realization makes obvious the futility of attachment to something that is so transitory. Thus the direct experience of *anicca* automatically gives rise to detachment, with which one can not only avert fresh reactions of craving or aversion, but also eliminate the very habit of reacting. In this way one gradually frees the mind of suffering. Unless its physical aspect is included, the awareness of *vedanā* remains partial and incomplete. Therefore the Buddha repeatedly emphasized the importance of the experience of impermanence through physical sensations. He said,

> Those who continually make efforts
> to direct their awareness toward the body,
> who abstain from unwholesome actions
> and strive to do what should be done,
> such people, aware, with full understanding,
> are freed from their defilements.[5]

The cause of suffering is *taṇhā,* craving and aversion. Ordinarily it appears to us that we generate reactions of craving and aversion toward the various objects that we encounter through the physical senses and the mind. The Buddha, however, discovered that between the object and the reaction stands a missing link: *vedanā.* We react not to the exterior reality but to the sensations within us. When we learn to observe sensation without reacting in craving and aversion, the cause of suffering does not arise, and suffering ceases. Therefore observation of *vedanā* is essential in order to practice what the Buddha taught. And the observation must be at the level of physical sensation if the awareness of *vedanā* is to be complete. With the awareness of physical sensation we can penetrate to the root of the problem and remove it. We can observe our own nature to the depths and can liberate ourselves from suffering.

By understanding the central importance of the observation of sensation in the teaching of the Buddha, one can gain fresh insight into the *Satipaṭṭhāna Sutta.*[6] The discourse begins by stating the aims of *satipaṭṭhāna,* of establishing awareness: "the purification of beings; the transcending of sorrow and lamentation; the extinguishing of physical and mental suffering; the practicing of a way of truth; the direct experience of the ultimate reality, *nibbāna.*"[7] It then briefly explains how to achieve these goals: "Here a meditator dwells ardent with thorough understanding and awareness, observing body in body, observing sensations in sensations, observing mind in mind, observing the contents of the mind in the contents of the mind, having abandoned craving and aversion toward the world."[8]

What is meant by "observing body in body, sensations in sensations," and so forth? For a Vipassana meditator, the expression is luminous in its clarity. Body, sensations, mind, and mental contents are the four dimensions of a human being. To understand this human phenomenon correctly, each of us must experience the reality of ourselves directly. To achieve this direct experience, the meditator must develop two qualities: awareness (**sati**) and thorough understanding (**sampajañña**). The discourse is called "The Establishing of Awareness," but awareness is incomplete without understanding, insight into the depths of one's own nature, into the impermanence of this phenomenon that one calls "I." The practice of *satipaṭṭhāna* leads the meditators to realize their essentially ephemeral nature. When they have had this personal realization, then awareness is firmly established—right awareness leading to liberation. Then automatically craving and aversion disappear, not just toward the external world but also toward the world within, where craving and aversion are most deep-seated, and most often overlooked—in the unthinking, visceral attachment to one's own body and mind. So long as this underlying attachment remains, one cannot be liberated from suffering.

The "Discourse on the Establishing of Awareness" first discusses observation of the body. This is the most apparent aspect of the mental-physical structure, and hence the proper point from which to begin the work of self-observation. From here observation of sensations, of mind, and of mental contents naturally develops. The discourse explains several ways to begin observing the body. The first and most common is awareness of respiration. Another way to begin is by giving attention to bodily movements. But no matter how one starts the journey, there are certain stages through which one must pass on the way to the final goal. These are described in a paragraph of crucial importance in the discourse:

In this way he dwells observing body in body internally or externally, or both internally and externally. He dwells observing the phenomenon of arising in the body. He dwells observing the phenomenon of passing away in the body. He dwells observing the phenomenon of arising and passing away in the body. Now the awareness presents itself to him, "This is body." This awareness develops to such an extent that only understanding and observation remain, and he dwells detached without clinging to anything in the world.[9]

The great importance of this passage is shown by the fact that it is repeated not only at the end of each section within the discussion of observation of the body, but also within the succeeding divisions of the discourse dealing with the observation of sensations, of mind, and of mental contents. (In these three later divisions, the word "body" is replaced by "sensations," "mind," and "mental contents" respectively.) The passage thus describes the common ground in the practice of *satipaṭṭhāna*. Because of the difficulties it presents, its interpretation has varied widely. However, the difficulties disappear when the passage is understood as referring to the awareness of sensations. In practicing *satipaṭṭhāna*, meditators must achieve a comprehensive insight into the nature of themselves. The means to this penetrating insight is the observation of sensations, including as it does the observation of the other three dimensions of the human phenomenon. Therefore although the first steps may differ, beyond a certain point the practice must involve awareness of sensation.

Hence, the passage explains, meditators begin by observing sensations arising in the interior of the body or externally, on the surface of the body, or both together. That is, from awareness of sensations in some parts and not in others, they gradually develop the ability to feel sensations throughout the body. When they begin the practice, they may first experience sensations of an intense nature which arise and seem to persist for some time. Meditators are aware of their arising, and after some time of their passing away. In this stage they are still experiencing the apparent reality of body and mind, their integrated, seemingly solid and lasting nature. But as one continues practicing, a stage is reached in which the solidity dissolves spontaneously, and mind and body are experienced in their true nature as a mass of vibrations, arising and passing away every moment. With this experience now one understands at last what body, sensations, mind, and mental contents really are: a flux of impersonal, constantly changing phenomena.

This direct apprehension of the ultimate reality of mind and matter progressively shatters one's illusions, misconceptions, and preconceptions. Even right conceptions that had been accepted only on faith or by intellectual deduction now acquire new significance when they are experienced. Gradually, by the observation of reality within, all the conditioning that distorts perception is eliminated. Only pure awareness and wisdom remain.

As ignorance disappears, the underlying tendencies of craving and aversion are eradicated, and the meditator becomes freed from all attachments—the deepest attachment being to the inner world of one's own body and mind. When this attachment is eliminated, suffering disappears and one becomes liberated.

The Buddha often said, "Whatever is felt is related to suffering."[10] Therefore *vedanā* is an ideal means to explore the truth of suffering. Unpleasant sensations are obviously suffering, but the most pleasant sensation is also a form of very subtle agitation. Every sensation is impermanent. If one is attached to pleasant sensations, then when they pass away, suffering remains. Thus every sensation contains a seed of misery. For this reason, as he spoke of the path leading to the cessation of suffering, the Buddha spoke of the path leading to the arising of *vedanā,* and that leading to its ceasing.[11] So long as one remains within the conditioned field of mind and matter, sensations and suffering persist. They cease only when one transcends that field to experience the ultimate reality of *nibbāna.*

The Buddha said:

> A man does not really apply Dhamma in life
> just because he speaks much about it.
> But though someone may have heard little about it,
> if he sees the Law of Nature by means of his own body,
> then truly he lives according to it,
> and can never be forgetful of the Dhamma.[12]

Our own bodies bear witness to the truth. When meditators discover the truth within, it becomes real for them and they live according to it. We can each realize that truth by learning to observe the sensations within ourselves, and by doing so we can attain liberation from suffering.

Appendix B

PASSAGES ON *VEDANĀ*
FROM THE *SUTTAS*

In his discourses the Buddha frequently referred to the importance of awareness of sensation. Here is a small selection of passages on this subject.

Through the sky blow many different winds, from east and west, from north and south, dust-laden or dustless, cold or hot, fierce gales or gentle breezes—many winds blow. In the same way, in the body sensations arise, pleasant, unpleasant, or neutral. When a meditator, practicing ardently, does not neglect his faculty of thorough understanding [*sampajañña*], then such a wise person fully comprehends sensations. Having fully comprehended them, he becomes freed from all impurities in this very life. At life's end, such a person, being established in Dhamma and understanding sensations perfectly, attains the indescribable stage beyond the conditioned world.
—S. XXXVI (II). ii. 12 (2), *Paṭhama Ākāsa Sutta*

And how does a meditator dwell observing body in body? In this case a meditator goes to the forest, to the foot of a tree, or to a solitary abode. There he sits down cross-legged with body erect, and fixes his attention in the area around the mouth. With awareness he breathes in and breathes out. Breathing in a long breath he knows rightly, "I am breathing in a long breath." Breathing out a long breath he knows rightly, "I am breathing out a long breath." Breathing in a short breath he knows rightly, "I am breathing in a short breath." Breathing out a short breath he knows rightly, "I am breathing out a short breath." "Feeling the entire body I shall breathe in"; thus he trains himself. "Feeling the entire body I shall breathe out"; thus he trains himself. "With bodily activities calmed I shall breathe in"; thus he trains himself. "With bodily activities calmed, I shall breathe out"; thus he trains himself.
—D. 22/M. 10, *Satipaṭṭhāna Sutta, Ānāpāna-pabbam*

When a sensation arises in the meditator, pleasant, unpleasant, or neutral, he understands, "A pleasant, unpleasant, or neutral sensation has arisen in me. It is based on something, it not without a base. On what is it based? On this very body." Thus he abides observing the impermanent nature of the sensation within the body.
—S. XXXVI (II). i. 7, Paṭhama Gelañña Sutta

The meditator understands, "There has arisen in me this pleasant, unpleasant, or neutral experience. It is composed, of a gross nature, dependent on conditions. But what really exists, what is most excellent, is equanimity." Whether a pleasant experience has arisen in him, or an unpleasant, or a neutral one, it ceases, but equanimity remains.
—M. 152, Indriya Bhāvanā Sutta

There are three types of sensation: pleasant, unpleasant, and neutral. All three are impermanent, composed, dependent on conditions, subject to decay, to decline, to fading away, to ceasing. Seeing this reality, the well-instructed follower of the Noble Path becomes equanimous toward pleasant, unpleasant, and neutral sensations. By developing equanimity, he becomes detached; by developing detachment, he becomes liberated.
—M. 74, Dīghanaka Sutta

If a meditator abides observing the impermanence of pleasant sensation within the body, its decline, fading away and ceasing, and also observing his own relinquishing of attachment to such sensation, then his underlying conditioning of craving for pleasant sensation within the body is eliminated. If he abides observing the impermanence of unpleasant sensation within the body, then his underlying conditioning of aversion toward unpleasant sensation within the body is eliminated. If he abides observing the impermanence of neutral sensation within the body, then his underlying conditioning of ignorance toward neutral sensation within the body is eliminated.
—S. XXXVI (II). i. 7, Paṭhama Gelañña Sutta

When his underlying conditionings of craving for pleasant sensation, of aversion toward unpleasant sensation, and of ignorance toward neutral sensation are eradicated, the meditator is called one who is totally free of underlying conditionings, who has seen the truth, who has cut off all craving and aversion, who has broken all bondages, who has fully realized the illusory nature of the ego, who has made an end of suffering.
—S. XXXVI (II). i. 3, Pahāna Sutta

The view of reality as it is becomes his right view. Thought of reality as it is becomes his right thought. Effort toward reality as it is becomes his right effort. Awareness of reality as it is becomes his right awareness. Concentration on reality as it is becomes his right concentration. His actions of body and speech and his livelihood become truly purified. Thus the Noble Eightfold Path advances in him toward development and fulfillment.

—M. 149, *Mahā-Saḷāyatanika Sutta*

The faithful follower of the Noble Path makes efforts, and by persisting in his efforts becomes mindful, and by remaining mindful becomes concentrated, and by maintaining concentration develops right understanding, and by understanding rightly develops real faith, being confident in knowing, "Those truths of which before I had only heard, now I dwell having experienced them directly within the body, and I observe them with penetrating insight."

—S. XLVIII (IV). v. 10 (50), *Āpaṇa Sutta* (spoken by Sāriputta, chief disciple of the Buddha)

GLOSSARY OF PĀLI TERMS

I ncluded in this list are Pāli terms that appear in the text as well as some other terms of importance in the teaching of the Buddha.

ānāpāna. Respiration. **Ānāpāna-sati**—awareness of respiration.

anattā. Not self, egoless, without essence, without substance. One of the three basic characteristics of phenomena, along with **anicca** and **dukkha**.

anicca. Impermanent, ephemeral, changing. One of the three basic characteristics of phenomena, along with **anattā** and **dukkha**.

anusaya. The unconscious mind; latent, underlying conditioning; dormant mental impurity (also **anusaya-kilesa**).

arahant/arahat. Liberated being. One who has destroyed all impurities of the mind.

ariya. Noble; saintly person. One who has purified the mind to the point of having experienced ultimate reality (**nibbāna**).

ariya aṭṭhangika magga. The Noble Eightfold Path leading to liberation from suffering. It is divided into three trainings, namely—

    sīla. morality, purity of vocal and physical actions:

        sammā-vācā. right speech,

        sammā-kammanta. right actions,

        sammā-ājīva. right livelihood;

    samādhi. concentration, control of one's own mind:

        sammā-vāyāma. right effort,

samma-sati. right awareness,

samma-samadhi. right concentration;

pañña. wisdom, insight which totally purifies the mind:

samma-sankappa. right thought,

samma-ditthi. right understanding.

ariya sacca. Noble truth. The Four Noble Truths are (1) the truth of suffering; (2) the truth of the origin of suffering; (3) the truth of the cessation of suffering; (4) the truth of the path leading to the cessation of suffering.

bhanga. Dissolution. An important stage in the practice of Vipassana. The experience of the dissolution of the apparent solidity of the body into subtle vibrations that are continually arising and passing away.

bhavana. Mental development, meditation. The two divisions of **bhavana** are the development of tranquility (**samatha-bhavana**), corresponding to concentration of mind (**samadhi**), and the development of insight (**vipassana-bhavana**), corresponding to wisdom (**pañña**). Development of **samatha** will lead to the states of mental absorption; development of **vipassana** will lead to liberation.

bhavana-maya pañña. Experiential wisdom. See **pañña.**

bhikkhu. (Buddhist) monk; meditator. Feminine form **bhikkhuni**— nun.

Buddha. Enlightened person. One who has discovered the way to liberation, has practiced it, and has reached the final goal by his own efforts.

cinta-maya pañña. Intellectual wisdom. See **pañña.**

citta. Mind. **Cittanupassana**—observation of the mind. See **satipatthana.**

dhamma. Phenomenon; object of mind; nature; natural law; law of liberation, i.e., teaching of an enlightened person. **Dhammanupassana**—observation of the contents of the mind. See **satipatthana.** (Sanskrit **dharma.**)

dukkha. Suffering, unsatisfactoriness. One of the three basic characteristics of phenomena, along with **anatta** and **anicca.**

Gotama. Family name of the historical Buddha. (Sanskrit **Gautama.**)

Hīnayāna. Literally, "lesser vehicle." Term used for **Theravāda** Buddhism by those of other schools. Pejorative connotation.

jhāna. State of mental absorption or trance. There are eight such states which may be attained by the practice of **samādhi**, or **samatha-bhāvanā.** Cultivation of them brings tranquility and bliss, but does not eradicate the deepest-rooted mental defilements.

kalāpa. Smallest indivisible unit of matter.

kamma. Action, specifically an action performed by oneself which will have an effect on one's future. (Sanskrit **karma.**)

kāya. Body. **Kāyānupassanā**—observation of the body. See **satipaṭṭhāna.**

Mahāyāna. Literally, "greater vehicle." The type of Buddhism that developed in India a few centuries after the Buddha and that spread north to Tibet, Mongolia, China, Viet Nam, Korea, and Japan.

mettā. Selfless love and good will. One of the qualities of a pure mind. **Mettā-bhāvanā**—the systematic cultivation of **mettā** by a technique of meditation.

nibbāna. Extinction; freedom from suffering; the ultimate reality; the unconditioned. (Sanskrit **nirvāṇa.**)

Pāli. Line; text. The texts recording the teaching of the Buddha; hence the language of these texts. Historical, linguistic, and archaeological evidence indicate that Pāli was a language actually spoken in northern India at or near the time of the Buddha. Later the texts were translated into Sanskrit, which was exclusively a literary language.

paññā. Wisdom. The third of the three trainings by which the Noble Eightfold Path is practiced (see **ariya aṭṭhangika magga**). There are three kinds of wisdom: **suta-mayā paññā**—literally, "wisdom gained from listening to others," i.e., received wisdom; **cintā-mayā paññā**—wisdom gained by intellectual analysis; and **bhāvanā-mayā paññā**—wisdom developing from direct, personal experience. Of these, only the last can totally purify the mind; it is cultivated by the practice of **vipassanā-bhāvanā.**

paticca–samuppāda. The Chain of Conditioned Arising; causal genesis. The process, beginning with ignorance, by which one keeps making life after life of suffering for oneself.

samādhi. Concentration, control of one's own mind. The second of the three trainings by which the Noble Eightfold Path is practiced (see **ariya atthangika magga**). When cultivated as an end in itself, it leads to the attainment of the states of mental absorption (**jhāna**), but not to total liberation of the mind.

sammā-sati. Right awareness. See **sati**.

sampajañña. Understanding of the totality of the human phenomenon, i.e., insight into its impermanent nature at the level of sensations.

samsāra. Cycle of rebirth; conditioned world; world of suffering.

sangha. Congregation; community of **ariyas**, i.e., those who have experienced **nibbāna**; community of Buddhist monks or nuns; a member of the **ariya-sangha**, **bhikkhu-sangha**, or **bhikkhunī-sangha**.

sankhāra. (Mental) formation; volitional activity; mental reaction; mental conditioning. One of the four aggregates or processes of the mind, along with **viññāna**, **saññā**, and **vedanā**. (Sanskrit **samskāra**.)

sankhāra-upekkhā/sankhārupekkhā. Literally, equanimity toward the **sankhāras**. A stage in the practice of Vipassana, subsequent to the experience of **bhanga**, in which old impurities lying dormant in the unconscious rise to the surface level of the mind, manifesting themselves as physical sensations. By maintaining equanimity (**upekkhā**) toward these sensations, the meditator creates no new **sankhāras**, and allows the old ones to be eradicated. Thus the process gradually leads to the eradication of all **sankhāras**.

saññā. Perception, recognition. One of the four mental aggregates or processes, along with **vedanā**, **viññāna**, and **sankhāra**. It is ordinarily conditioned by one's past **sankhāras**, and therefore conveys a distorted image of reality. In the practice of Vipassana, **saññā** is changed into **paññā**, the understanding of reality as it is. It becomes **anicca-saññā**, **dukkha-saññā**, **anattā-saññā**, **asubha-**

saññā—that is, the perception of impermanence, suffering, egolessness, and the illusory nature of beauty.

sati. Awareness. **Ānāpāna-sati**—awareness of respiration. **Sammā-sati**—right awareness, a constituent of the Noble Eightfold Path (see **ariya aṭṭhangika magga**).

satipaṭṭhāna. the establishing of awareness. There are four interconnected aspects of **satipaṭṭhāna**: (1) observation of the body (**kāyānupassanā**); (2) observation of sensations arising within the body (**vedanānupassanā**); (3) observation of the mind (**cittānupassanā**); (4) observation of the contents of the mind (**dhammanupassanā**). All four are included in the observation of sensations, since sensations are directly related to both body and mind.

Siddhattha. Literally, "one who has accomplished his task." The personal name of the historical Buddha. (Sanskrit **Siddhārtha**.)

sīla. Morality, abstaining from physical and vocal actions that cause harm to others and oneself. The first of the three trainings by which the Noble Eightfold Path is practiced (see **ariya aṭṭhangika magga**).

suta-mayā paññā. Received wisdom. See **paññā**.

sutta. Discourse of the Buddha or one of his leading disciples. (Sanskrit **sūtra**).

taṇhā. Literally, "thirst." Includes both craving and its reverse image of aversion. The Buddha identified **taṇhā** as the cause of suffering in his first sermon, the "Discourse Setting in Motion the Wheel of Dhamma" (**Dhamma-cakkappavattana Sutta**). In the Chain of Conditioned Arising, he explained that **taṇhā** originates as a reaction to sensation (see above, p. 49).

tathāgata. Literally "thus-gone" or "thus-come." One who by walking on the path of reality has reached the ultimate reality, i.e., an enlightened person. The term by which the Buddha commonly referred to himself.

Theravāda. Literally, "teaching of the elders." The teachings of the Buddha, in the form in which they have been preserved in the countries of South Asia (Burma, Sri Lanka, Thailand, Laos, Cambodia). Generally recognized as the oldest form of the teachings.

Tipiṭaka. Literally, "three baskets." The three collections of the teachings of the Buddha, namely: (1) **Vinaya-piṭaka**—the collection of monastic discipline; (2) **Sutta-piṭaka**—the collection of discourses; (3) **Abhidhamma-piṭaka**—"the collection of higher teaching," i.e., systematic philosophical exegesis of the Dhamma. (Sanskrit **Tripiṭaka.**)

vedanā. Sensation. One of the four mental aggregates or processes, along with **viññāṇa, saññā,** and **sankhāra.** Described by the Buddha as having both mental and physical aspects; therefore **vedanā** offers a means to examine the totality of mind and body. In the Chain of Conditioned Arising, the Buddha explained that **taṇhā,** the cause of suffering, originates as a reaction to **vedanā** (see above, 49). By learning to observe **vedanā** objectively, one can avoid any new reactions of craving or aversion, and can experience directly within oneself the reality of impermanence (**anicca**). This experience is essential for the development of detachment, leading to liberation of the mind. **Vedanānupassanā**—observation of sensations within the body. See **satipaṭṭhāna.**

viññāṇa. Consciousness, cognition. One of the four mental aggregates or processes, along with **saññā, vedanā,** and **sankhāra.**

vipassanā. Introspection, insight that totally purifies the mind. Specifically, insight into the impermanent nature of mind and body. **Vipassanā-bhāvanā**—the systematic development of insight through the meditation technique of observing the reality of oneself by observing sensations within the body.

yathā-bhūta. Literally, "as it is." Reality.

yathā-bhūta-ñāṇa-dassana. Wisdom arising from seeing the truth as it is.

NOTES

All quotations are from the *Sutta Pitaka*, the *Collection of Discourses* of the Pāli Canon. The Pāli text followed here is that published in Devanagari script by Nalanda University, Bihar, India. English translations consulted include those of the Pāli Text Society of London, as well as those printed by the Buddhist Publication Society of Sri Lanka. I have found particularly valuable the anthologies prepared by Vens. Ñānatiloka, Ñānamoli, and Piyadassi. To them and to the other modern translators of the Pāli Canon I am deeply indebted.

The numbering of the *suttas* given in the notes is that used in the English translations of the Pāli Text Society. In general, titles of *suttas* have been left untranslated.

The following abbreviations have been used:

A—*Anguttara Nikāya*
D—*Dīgha Nikāya*
M—*Majjhima Nikāya*
S—*Samyutta Nikāya*
Satip—*Satipaṭṭhāna Sutta* (D. 22, M. 10)

Chapter 1

1. S. XLIV. x. 2, *Anurādha Sutta*.
2. A. III. vii. 65, *Kesamutti Sutta (Kālāma Sutta)*, iii, ix.
3. D. 16, *Mahā-Parinibbāna Suttanta*.
4. Ibid.
5. S. XXII. 87 (5), *Vakkali Sutta*.
6. *Mahā-Parinibbāna Suttanta*.
7. A. IV. v. 5 (45), *Rohitassa Sutta*. Also found in S. II. iii. 6.
8. *Dhammapada*, I. 19 & 20.
9. Based on M. 107, *Ganaka-Mogallāna Sutta*.

Chapter 2

1. *Sankhāra* is one of the most important concepts in the teaching of the Buddha, and one of the most difficult to express in English. The word also has multiple meanings, and it may not be readily apparent which meaning applies in a particular context. Here *sankhāra* is taken as equivalent to *cetanā/sañcetanā*, meaning will, volition, intention. For this interpretation see A. IV. xviii. 1 (171), *Cetanā Sutta*; S. XXII. 57 (5), *Sattatthāna Sutta*; S. XII. iv. 38 (8), *Cetanā Sutta*.
2. M. 72, *Aggi-Vacchagotta Sutta*.

Chapter 3

1. M. 135, *Cūḷa Kamma Vibhanga Sutta.*
2. *Dhammapada,* XXV. 21 (380).
3. Ibid, I. 1 & 2.
4. *Sutta Nipāta,* III. 12, *Dvayatānupassanā Sutta.*
5. S. LVI (XII). ii. 1, *Dhamma-cakkappavattana Sutta.*
6. A. III. xiii. 130, *Lekha Sutta.*
7. Based on A. I. xvii, *Eka Dhamma Pāli* (2).

Chapter 4

1. S. LVI (XII). ii. 1, *Dhamma-cakkappavattana Sutta.*
2. Ibid.
3. M. 38, *Mahā-taṇhāsankhaya Sutta.*
4. Ibid.
5. Ibid.
6. *Dhammapada,* XII. 9 (165).
7. D. 9, *Poṭṭhapāda Suttanta.*
8. A. III. vii. 65, *Kesamutti Sutta (Kālāma Sutta),* xvi.
9. Based on S. XLII. viii. 6, *Asibandhakaputta Sutta.*

Chapter 5

1. *Dhammapada,* XIV. 5 (183).
2. Ibid., I. 17 & 18.
3. M. 27, *Cūḷa-hatthi-padopama Sutta.*
4. Ibid.

Chapter 6

1. A. IV. ii. 3 (13), *Padhāna Sutta.*

Chapter 7

1. *Dhammapada,* XXIV. 5 (338).
2. D. 16, *Mahā-Parinibbāna Suttanta.*
3. *Dhammapada,* XX. 4 (276).
4. See S. XLVI (II). vi. 2, *Pariyāya Sutta.*
5. S. XII. vii. 62 (2), *Dutiya Assutavā Sutta;* also S. XXXVI (II). i. 10, *Phassa Mūlaka Sutta.*
6. *Dhammapada,* XX. 5 (277).
7. S. XXXVI (II). i. 7, *Paṭhama Gelañña Sutta.*

Chapter 8

1. D. 16, *Mahā-Parinibbāna Suttanta.* The verse is spoken by Sakka, king of the gods, after the passing of the Buddha. It appears in slightly different form elsewhere. See, for example, S. I. ii. 1, *Nandana Sutta;* also S. IX. 6, *Anuruddha Sutta.*
2. A. IX. ii. 10 (20), *Velāma Sutta.*
3. The famous simile of the raft is taken from M. 22, *Alagaddūpama Sutta.*
4. Based on *Udāna,* I. x, story of Bāhiya Dārucīriya. Also found in *Dhammapada Commentary,* VIII. 2 (verse 101).

Chapter 9

1. S. LVI (XII). ii. 1, *Dhamma-cakkappavattana Sutta.* This formula is used to describe the insight attained by the earliest disciples on first realizing the Dhamma.

2. S. v. 7, *Upacālā Sutta.* The speaker is the *arahat* nun Upacālā.
3. *Dhammapada,* XXV. 15 (374).
4. *Udāna,* VIII. 1.
5. *Udāna,* VIII. 3.
6. S. LVI (XII). ii. 1, *Dhamma-cakkappavattana Sutta.*
7. S. XXXVIII (IV). 1, *Nibbāna Pañhā Sutta.* The speaker is Sāriputta, chief disciple of the Buddha.
8. *Sutta Nipāta,* II. 4, *Mahā-Mangala Sutta.*
9. D. 9, *Poṭṭhapāda Suttanta.*

Chapter 10
1. *Dhammapada,* VIII. 14 (113).
2. S. XXII. 102 (10), *Anicca-saññā Sutta.*
3. D. 16, *Mahā-Parinibbāna Suttanta.*
4. M. 117, *Mahā-cattārīsaka Sutta.*
5. Ibid.

Appendix A: The Importance of Vedanā *in the Teaching of the Buddha*
1. A. VIII. ix. 3 (83), *Mūlaka Sutta.* See also A. IX. ii. 4 (14), *Samiddhi Sutta.*
2. D. 1.
3. A. III. vii. 61 (ix), *Titthāyatana Sutta.*
4. S. XXXVI (II). iii. 22 (2), *Aṭṭhasata Sutta.*
5. *Dhammapada,* XXI. 4 (293).
6. The *Satipaṭṭhāna Sutta* appears twice in the *Sutta Piṭaka,* at D. 22 and at M. 10. In the D. version, the section discussing *dhammānupassanā* is longer than in the M. version. Therefore the D. text is referred to as the *Mahā-Satipaṭṭhāna Suttanta,* "the greater." Otherwise the two texts are identical. The passages quoted in this work appear in the same form in both texts.
7. *Satip.*
8. Ibid.
9. Ibid.
10. S. XII. iv. 32 (2), *Kaḷāra Sutta.*
11. S. XXXVI (II). iii. 23 (3), *Aññatara Bhikkhu Sutta.*
12. *Dhammapada,* XIX. 4 (259).

ADDRESSES

Courses in Vipassana meditation as taught by S. N. Goenka are held regularly in North America, Europe, Australia, and Japan, as well as in India and neighboring countries. Information is available from the following permanent centers:

Vipassana Meditation Center
P.O. Box 24
Shelburne Falls, MA 01370
U.S.A.   Telephone: (413) 625-2160

Vipassana Meditation Centre
P.O. Box 103
Blackheath, NSW 2785
Australia   Telephone: (047) 877 436

Vipassana International Academy
Dhammagiri, Igatpuri (District Nasik)
Maharashtra 422 403
India   Telephone: Igatpuri 76